A COMPLETE IDENTIFICATION GUIDE TO THE

WURLITZER JUKEBOX

JUKEBOX COLLECTOR NEWSLETTER
2545 S.E. 60TH COURT
DES MOINES, IOWA 50317-5099

RICK BOTTS

ACKNOWLEDGEMENTS

Deutsche Wurlitzer GmbH
Hans Domberg
Norbert Lohre
Werner Schulz
George Seidel
Klaus Telgheder

The Wurlitzer Company
Robert W. Donaldson
Stan Grajek
Carol Houghtby
Gary Hurt
Joseph Kocsis

C and K Printing (Printer)
Carl Schnoebelen
Jim Laird
Thao Van Nguyen

Production Advisiors
Barb Botts
Steve Loots
Gary Shaw

Ampersand (Typesetting)

Custom Camera (Color Separations)

Rod Caudle Photography (Cover photograph)
Rod Caudle, Atlanta, GA.

Jeff Horn Creative Designs (Designer of cover and interior layout)
Jeff Horn

LIBRARY OF CONGRESS CATALOG
CARD NUMBER 83-82604

ISBN 0-912789-01-8

PUBLISHED BY:

JUKEBOX COLLECTOR NEWSLETTER
2545 SE 60TH COURT
DES MOINES, IOWA 50317-5099
515-265-8324

For more information about the current Wurlitzer models, contact -

Jerry Reeves
503 W. Central Blvd.
Orlando, Fl. 32801
Phone: 305-843-4302

Deutsche Wurlitzer GmbH
Box 1251
D-4971 Hullhorst, West Germany
Phone: 05744-5050

ABOUT THE LISTINGS

I've tried to keep the listings in this book useful and simple. If I couldn't document the information, I left the listing blank rather than provide you with erroneous information. I'll continue to look for the facts and figures to fill in the missing blanks. If you would like to help, I would be happy to hear from you.

MODEL

The 1017, 1017-A and 1217 are the only hideaway models listed in this book. The reason for this is there were small production runs of the other hideaway models and only a nominal interest in collecting hideaways.

When optional features became available, such as Top Tune, LP, etc., the model numbers were expanded to reflect these options or option packages. For example, there are 10 versions of the 3800. One version is the 3800-1AD. The 1AD identifies the option package that was incorporated into the 3800. I did not expand the model listings to include all of these optional package versions.

YEAR OF SHIPMENT

The years of shipment were obtained from official Wurlitzer records. Instead of using the model year, I used the year of shipment. Especially during the early 40's, this more accurately describes what happened. For instance if you believed the "What's New for 42" brochure, you would be wrong. The only machine in the '42 brochure that was shipped in 1942 was the Wurlitzer 950.

PICTURES

All the pictures used in this book, with the exception of 3, were obtained from black and white or color glossies belonging to The Wurlitzer Company or from original Wurlitzer advertising brochures. The pictures of the machines are exact or very close to an actual machine depending on a machines stage of development when photographed. Keep in mind, especially in the 30's and 40's with many different models under development at the same time, many of the pictures were taken before a machine was ready for production, in order to meet the advertising department's deadlines.

Also, keep in mind, in the late 30's and in the 40's there were companies that sold kits to modify jukeboxes. If you find a Wurlitzer that is much different in appearance than these pictured in this book, you do not have a Wurlitzer prototype that is very valuable because it somehow got out of the factory and into your hands. What you have is a Wurlitzer cabinet modified by a kit or a new cabinet from an independent supplier, with a Wurlitzer mech., amp., etc. inserted inside the new cabinet.

MISCELLANEOUS

Most of the miscellaneous information came from Wurlitzer advertising brochures or service manuals. Some of you know the Wurlitzer 1015 inside-out, while others of you know the 1800, 2400, 3200, etc. inside-out. No one is an expert on every model, but you may be an expert on a particular model. With your help I can make the miscellaneous section more informative and useful.

DIMENSIONS

The dimensions listed could vary a little depending on who is reading the tape measure. Wurlitzer service manuals, advertising brochures and ads weren't always in agreement with each other.

As an example, in measuring a jukebox, do you measure the wood cabinet or do you take into account the metal castings attached to the cabinet? The jukebox may or may not go through the door if you believe all the dimensions as gospel.

WEIGHT

These figures were taken from Wurlitzer service manuals or brochures and, as with the dimensions, they can vary depending on who or how the machine is weighed. Also any options added to the machine could change the weight.

AMPLIFIER

The amplifier numbers were obtained from Wurlitzer service and parts manuals. The norm in the USA today is 110 volt - 60 cycle electricity, so only those amplifiers are listed. There were many other models of Wurlitzer amplifiers manufactured but they are rarely found in the USA because they were designed for direct current, 220 volt, 25 or 50 cycle alternating current, etc. If you have a non-listed amplifier, I'll be happy to identify the machine it belongs to if you would drop me a post card.

CORRECTIONS

On page 53, the picture is a 2304
On page 54, the picture is a 2404
On page 55, the picture is a 2250

RICK BOTTS

WURLITZER JUKEBOXES

North Tonawanda, New York, was the home of the Wurlitzer coin-operated phonograph factory until 1974. The P-10 through the 3800 series were made at North Tonawanda. In 1974 Wurlitzer ceased production at North Tonawanda but a Wurlitzer subsidiary (Wurlitzer G.m.b.H.) continued to produce jukeboxes in Germany.

Wurlitzer G.m.b.H. has been making phonographs in Germany since the early 60's. This was done mainly to protect its sales to the Common Market countries. Since 1974, Germany has been responsible for engineering, production and world-wide marketing of all coin-operated Wurlitzer products.

Model	year of shipment	picture on page	number of selections	miscellaneous	Dimensions H x W x D	weight	amp. number
Debutante	1933	6	10	The test model used by Wurlitzer to determine if jukeboxes would sell. It does not have the Wurlitzer name on it.	—	—	3314, 3414
P-10	1934-35	7	10	The 1st model from Wurlitzer with the Wurlitzer name on it.	48½ x 30¼ x 20¾	—	6067A-3, 6067A3-2, 453, 399, 368-A
P-20	1934-35	8	10		47 x 33 x 22	—	399, 368-A 6067A-3
P-12	1935	9	12		49 x 33 x 22¾	—	550
P-400	1935	10	12		51½ x 36 x 24	—	570
P-30	1935	11	12		49½ x 30¼ x 21½	—	551
35	1936	12	12	It has a very wide cabinet. Nicknamed "Jumbo."	56⅜ x 44½ x 24	—	680
312	1936	13	12		51 x 31⅜ x 22¼	—	660,661,
412	1936	14	12		49 x 33 x 22¾	—	660,661
400	1936	15	12				671, 672
316	1937	—	16	This is the same cabinet as the 312.	51 x 31⅜ x 22¼	—	771
416	1937	—	16	This is the same cabinet as the 412.	49 x 33 x 22¾	—	771
616	1937	16	16		51⅜ x 31⅜ x 22	—	771
616-A	1937	17	16	It is the same as the 616, except it has horizontal "Lucite" bars in the grille. The 1st use of "Lucite" in a jukebox.	51⅜ x 31⅜ x 22	—	771
716	1937	18	16		51⅛ x 31⅜ x 22¼	—	771
24	1938	19	24	The 1st Wurlitzer with plastics.	52 x 31 x 25	310	851
24-A	1938	—	24	The "A" model is identical to the 24 except it is equipped with magnetic selectors, butterfly switches, Wurlitzer coin entry slides and a built-in scavenger cup. This is a better coin mechanism.	52 x 31 x 25	310	851

Model	year of shipment	picture on page	number of selections	miscellaneous	Dimensions H x W x D	weight	amp. number
G-500	1938-39	22	24	The G model has moving grille colors, red pilaster plastics and onyx grille plastics.	58⅝ x 35 x 28¼	410	854
G-500-A	1938-39	—	24	Same as G-500 except has "A" equipment. (See 24-A).	58⅝ x 35 x 28¼	410	854
P-500	1938-39	—	24	This is the most common version of the 500 series. Model P has moving pilaster colors, onyx pilaster plastics and red grille plastics. This is the reverse of the G-500.	58⅝ x 35 x 28¼	410	854
P-500-A	1938-39	—	24	Same as the P-500 except has "A" equipment (See 24-A).	58⅝ x 35 x 28¼	410	854
600	1938-39	20	24	The economy model with rotary selector.	53⅞ x 30⅞ x 24⅛	336	851
600-A	1938-39	—	24	Same as 600 except has "A" equipment (See 24-A).	53⅞ x 30⅞ x 24⅛	336	851
K-600	1939	21	24	Same as 600 except has keyboard selector (K).	53⅞ x 30⅞ x 24⅛	336	851
K-600-A	1939	—	24	Same as K-600 except has "A" equipment (See 24-A).	53⅞ x 30⅞ x 24⅛	336	851
50	1938	23	12	A model 51 mechanism in a slender floor model. Nicknamed "Console".	47½ x 23¼ x 17¾	165	752
51	1938	24	12	The 1st Wurlitzer countertop.	20 x 27½ x 18½	120	741
61	1938-39	25	12	The 1st Wurlitzer countertop with plastics.	22 x 21¼ x 18	115	841
41	1940	26	12	The smallest of the Wurlitzer countertops.	17 x 21¼ x 18⅞	105	041
41-H	1940	—	12	41 with no coin mechanism.	17 x 21¼ x 18⅞	101	041
71	1940	27*	12	*The picture is of an 81, but the 71 is nearly identical. The 71 is a deluxe countertop model. It takes nickels, dimes and quarters. It has yellow plastics.	23⅛ x 22¼ x 19⅝	146	071
81	1941	27	12	Same as the 71 countertop except it has orange marbled plastics and highly figured Oriental Walnut & Myrtle Burl veneer.	23⅛ x 22¼ x 19⅝	146	071
700	1940	28	24	The economy model for 1940.	56½ x 32 x 25½	357	700
800	1940	28	24	The 1st Wurlitzer with bubble tubes. It also has revolving color cylinders.	61 x 37 x 27¾	428	800
750	1941	29	24	It has the mechanical keyboard selector.	55¾ x 32 x 26	308	501
750-E	1941	—	24	The 1st Wurlitzer with the electric keyboard selector (E).	55¾ x 32 x 26	308	501
780	1940-41	30	24	Nicknamed "Colonial Model." Colonial models were of conservative design for the high-class locations. This version had the mechanical keyboard selector.	61 x 37¾ x 25¼	317	501
780-E	1940-41	—	24	Same as the 780 except the "E" indicates it has the electric keyboard selector.	61 x 37¾ x 25¼	317	501

Model	year of shipment	picture on page	number of selections	miscellaneous	Dimensions H x W x D	weight	amp. number
850	1941	31	24	An expensive model then and today. It is nicknamed the "Peacock." Polaroid illumination provides ever-changing colors on the peacock glass.	65½ x 39 x 26½	410	501
850-A	1941	—	24	Same as the 850, except the peacock glass was replaced with tulip glass (as found in the Wurlitzer 580 speaker) & has no polarizing unit.	65½ x 39 x 26½	400	501
950	1942	32	24	The 1st Wurlitzer to use fluorescent lighting.	61¾ x 36$\frac{9}{16}$ x 25⅞	369	501
42 "Victory"	1942-45	33	12,16,24 (usually 24)	World War II model. Nicknamed "Victory." A reconditioned chassis (usually a 24, 24-A, 600 or 600K, but you may find that others were also used) in a new cabinet. It comes in a rotary or keyboard model.	65½ x 41 x 27	varies	various
1015	1946-47	34 & cover pages	24	This is the all-time sales leader. 56,246 were shipped. It has 8 bubble tubes and 2 revolving color cylinders for animation.	59⅞ x 33½ x 25	360	503
1017	1946-47	35	24	A hideaway model or concealed model, this unit is mechanically the same as a 1015. Wallboxes are used to make the record selections.	31½ x 30 x 21	—	503
1017-A	1947-48	—	24	An improved hideaway, incorporating the Zenith Cobra Tonearm.	31½ x 31½ x 23	235	227
1080	1947	36	24	Nicknamed "Colonial Model." It is mechanically the same as a 1015. Five mirrored plastics accent the cabinet.	58⅝ x 33⅜ x 25	350	503
1080-A	1947-48	—	24	This 1080 model incorporates the 1100 sound system and the Zenith Cobra Tonearm.	58⅝ x 33⅜ x 25	343	506
1080-C	1948	37	24	A 1080-A with different plastics, different grille cloth and incorporating a color animation unit in the grille. A rare model.	58⅝ x 33⅜ x 25	350	506
1100	1947-49	38	24	The 1100 was the first commercial phonograph to use the Zenith Cobra Tonearm. The 1st to introduce clear non-fade plastics. It was also the last model that Paul Fuller designed.	57⅞ x 30½ x 27¼	355	506
1217	1950-52	—	48	A hideaway version of the 1250.	—	—	512
1250	1950	39	48	This model still holds 24 records but plays 48 selections because it has a Dual Cobra Pickup. It plays 78's but can be converted to 45's or 7" 33⅓ records in 30 minutes.	59⅜ x 36½ x 27⅞	380	510

Model	year of shipment	picture on page	number of selections	miscellaneous	Dimensions H x W x D	weight	amp. number
1400 & 1450	1951-52	40	48	A 78RPM machine that features 30 second change-over to 45RPM or 7" 33⅓ RPM. The 1400 "Deluxe" and the 1450 "Custom" were the same machine except for the cabinet finish. "Deluxe" is a walnut finish and "Custom" comes in Blue, Blonde, Brown, Red or Mahogany "Textileather" finish. The 1952 models were restyled some. The backdoor mural was changed to a moonlit water scene, the colors on the color cylinders were changed, the grille was restyled and 2 blue fluorescent tubes were added to the record compartment.	$57\frac{1}{8}$ x $34\frac{1}{2}$ x $27\frac{5}{8}$	350	514
1400-A & 1450-A	1953	—	—		—	—	—
1500 & 1550	1952-53	41	104	This model automatically plays 78's or 45's intermixed, thanks to the "Wurlimagic Brain." It can be converted to all 7" 33⅓ records. The 1500 "Deluxe" and the 1550 "Custom" are the same except for cabinet finish. "Deluxe" is a walnut finish. "Custom" is Blue, Blonde, Red or Mahogany "Textileather" finish.	$59\frac{5}{8}$ x $38\frac{1}{8}$ x $27\frac{7}{16}$	470	516
1500-A & 1550-A	1953-54	42	104	Updated version of the 1500 series. A new glass dome lid instead of plastic, new valance plastics, new grille, new golden backdoor background and much-needed mechanical improvements.	$56\frac{1}{4}$ x $38\frac{1}{8}$ x $27\frac{7}{16}$	455	520
1500AF	1953-54	—	—	—	—	—	—
1600	1953	—	48	Plays 78's with a quick changeover to 45's possible or it can be adapted to 33⅓. The 1600 "Deluxe" has a walnut finish. The 1600 "Custom" has a Blue, Blonde, Red or Mahogany "Vinyl Plastic" finish.	$55\frac{1}{4}$ x $33\frac{1}{8}$ x 28	350	518
1650	1953	43	48	Plays only 45's. The cabinet finishes are the same as their respective 1600 models.	$55\frac{1}{4}$ x $33\frac{1}{8}$ x 28	350	518
1600A	1953-54	—	48	Plays 78's or 45's. It has a dark walnut finish and standard sound system.	$53\frac{1}{2}$ x $29\frac{3}{8}$ x $26\frac{7}{8}$	315	526
1600AF	1953-55	44	48	Plays 78's or 45's. Lime Walnut finish and Hi-Fi sound system.	$53\frac{1}{2}$ x $29\frac{3}{8}$ x $26\frac{7}{8}$	315	526HF
1650A	1954	—	48	Plays only 45's. It has a dark wanut finish and standard sound system.	$53\frac{1}{2}$ x $29\frac{3}{8}$ x $26\frac{7}{8}$	315	526
1650AF	1954	—	48	Plays only 45's. Lime Walnut finish and Hi-Fi sound system.	$53\frac{1}{2}$ x $29\frac{3}{8}$ x $26\frac{7}{8}$	315	526HF
1700	1954	—	104	This is the 1st Wurlitzer with the carousel record changer. It plays only 45's. It has a dark walnut cabinet and standard sound system.	$55\frac{1}{2}$ x $31\frac{7}{8}$ x $27\frac{1}{2}$	308	524
1700HF	1954	46	104	Same as the 1700 except it has a Lime Walnut cabinet and Hi-Fi sound system.	$55\frac{1}{2}$ x $31\frac{7}{8}$ x $27\frac{1}{2}$	308	524HF
1800	1955	47	104	It plays 45's and has a Hi-Fi sound system. Color of cabinet finishes are Dawn Mist, Horizon Blue, Sunset Red or Midnight Black.	$55\frac{1}{4}$ x $32\frac{1}{2}$ x $27\frac{3}{8}$	309	528HF
1900	1955-56	48	104	The 1st of the "Centennial Models." Color of cabinet finishes are Persian Turquoise, Glacier White, Chinese Black and Desert Haze.	$55\frac{5}{8}$ x $33\frac{11}{16}$ x $27\frac{7}{8}$	323	530

Model	year of shipment	picture on page	number of selections	miscellaneous	Dimensions H x W x D	weight	amp. number
2000	1956	49	200	The other "Centennial Model." It is nearly the same as the 1900, except it is the 1st Wurlitzer 200 play model. Consequently it has novel Roto-Page programs (revolving title strip holders). And as an option, another Wurlitzer 1st, the double coin entry accepting half dollars.	$55\frac{5}{8}$ x $33\frac{11}{16}$ x $27\frac{7}{8}$	375	530
2100	1957	—	200		$55\frac{5}{8}$ x $33\frac{5}{8}$ x $27\frac{7}{8}$	355	532
2104	1957	50	104		$55\frac{5}{8}$ x $33\frac{5}{8}$ x $27\frac{7}{8}$	323	532
2150	1957	51	200		$56\frac{3}{4}$ x $34\frac{1}{16}$ x $27\frac{1}{2}$	340	532
2200	1958	52	200		$53\frac{17}{32}$ x $35\frac{15}{16}$ x $27\frac{15}{16}$	364	532
2200-S	1958	—	200	S = stereo. Wurlitzer was 1st in adapting it to coin-operated phonographs.	$53\frac{17}{32}$ x $35\frac{15}{16}$ x $27\frac{15}{16}$	—	—
2204	1958	—	104		$53\frac{17}{32}$ x $35\frac{15}{16}$ x $27\frac{15}{16}$	324	532
2204-S	1958	—	104	A rare machine. Only one was shipped.	$53\frac{17}{32}$ x $35\frac{15}{16}$ x $27\frac{15}{16}$	—	—
2250	1958	53	200		$56\frac{1}{8}$ x $34\frac{1}{16}$ x $27\frac{1}{2}$	336	532
2300	1959	—	200	Monophonic Hi-Fi sound.	$51\frac{1}{2}$ x 34 x $27\frac{7}{8}$	324	536
2300-S	1959	—	200	Stereophonic Hi-Fi sound when used with auxiliary stereo speakers. It uses a new stereo pickup equipped with 2 built-in sapphire stylii. When 1 stylus becomes worn a lever flips the new stylus in place. The entire stylus is replaced with both stylus are worn.	$51\frac{1}{2}$ x 34 x $27\frac{7}{8}$	334	534
2304	1959	54	104	Mono.	$51\frac{1}{2}$ x 34 x $27\frac{7}{8}$	302	536
2304-S	1959	—	104	Stereo.	$51\frac{1}{2}$ x 34 x $27\frac{7}{8}$	312	538
2310	1959	—	100	Mono. The 1st 100 selection Wurlitzer.	$51\frac{1}{2}$ x 34 x $27\frac{7}{8}$	320	536
2310-S	1959	—	100	Stereo.	$51\frac{1}{2}$ x 34 x $27\frac{7}{8}$	$332\frac{1}{2}$	534
2400	1960	—	200	Hi-Fi monophonic sound.	$51\frac{1}{2}$ x 34 x $27\frac{7}{8}$	333	536
2400-S	1960	—	200	Hi-Fi stereophonic sound	$51\frac{1}{2}$ x 34 x $27\frac{7}{8}$	343	538
2404	1960	55	104	Mono.	$51\frac{1}{2}$ x 34 x $27\frac{7}{8}$	314	536
2404-S	1960	—	104	Stereo.	$51\frac{1}{2}$ x 34 x $27\frac{7}{8}$	317	538
2410	1960	—	100	Mono.	$51\frac{1}{2}$ x 34 x $27\frac{7}{8}$	316	536
2410-S	1960	—	100	Stereo.	$51\frac{1}{2}$ x 34 x $27\frac{7}{8}$	330	538

Model	year of shipment	picture on page	number of selections	miscellaneous	Dimensions H x W x D	weight	amp. number
2500	1961	56	200	Mono. The 2500's use a multipurpose sonotone pickup with dual 7/10 mil. sapphire stylus. It was standard on all models.	51½ x 34⅜ x 27⅞	332	540
2500-S	1961	—	200	Stereo	51½ x 34⅜ x 27⅞	—	542
2504	1961	—	104	Mono.	51½ x 34⅜ x 27⅞	318	540
2504-S	1961	—	104	Stereo.	51½ x 34⅜ x 27⅞	—	542
2510	1961	—	100	Mono.	51½ x 34⅜ x 27⅞	320	540
2510-S	1961	—	100	Stereo	51½ x 34⅜ x 27⅞	—	542
2600	1962	57	200	45RPM and 7" 33⅓ records can be intermixed. You get monographic sound from the phonograph but a throw-switch can change the sound to stereo by utilizing remote stereo speakers. As an option you can have a single button that actuates the top ten tunes for a 50¢ coin.	54 x 34¼ x 27⅞	340	543
2610	1962	—	100	See 2600.	54 x 34¼ x 27⅞	330	543
2700	1963	58	200	As an option, the top ten tunes are now operated by a golden selector bar by the coin insert.	54⅞ x 32¼ x 27⅝	332	544
2710	1963	—	100	See 2700.	54⅞ x 32¼ x 27⅝	317	544
2800	1964	59	200	A new option introduced with the 2800 was the Little LP feature. There were 3 songs on each side of the record.	52¼ x 33¾ x 27⅝	355	545
2810	1964	—	100	See 2800.	52¼ x 33¾ x 27⅝	340	545
2900	1965	60	200	New solid state amplifier.	51 x 33¾ x 27	350	546
2910	1965	—	100	For those who prefer blondes, the 2910-A blonde cabinet was available.	51 x 33¾ x 27	335	546
3000	1966	61	200		53½ x 35⅛ x 27	378	546B
3010	1966	—	100		53½ x 35⅛ x 27	363	546B
3100	1967	62	200	Called the "Americana," it introduced the optional "dollar bill accepter."	48 x 40 x 24½	367	547
3110	1967	—	100	See 3100.	48 x 40 x 24½	356	547
3200	1968	63	200	Called the "Americana II."	49 x 40¼ x 24⅝	378	548
3210	1968	—	100	See 3200.	49 x 40¼ x 24⅝	368	548
3300	1969	64	200	Called the "Americana III." It had animation in the panoramic panel.	53 x 40¼ x 23½	382	549
3310	1969	—	100	See 3300.	53 x 40¼ x 23½	372	549

Model	year of shipment	picture on page	number of selections	miscellaneous	Dimensions H x W x D	weight	amp. number
3400	1970	65	200	Called the "Statesman."	53 x $40\frac{7}{8}$ x 24	372	550
3410	1970	—	100	See 3400.	53 x $40\frac{7}{8}$ x 24	369	550
3460	1970	—	160	A new 160 play version was introduced. It matches most of the competitive 160 wallboxes.	53 x $40\frac{7}{8}$ x 24	369	550
3500	1971	66	200	Called the "Zodiac."	$52\frac{3}{4}$ x $40\frac{1}{4}$ x $25\frac{1}{4}$	375	551
3510	1971	—	100	See 3500.	$52\frac{3}{4}$ x $40\frac{1}{4}$ x $25\frac{1}{4}$	372	551
3560	1971	—	160	See 3500.	$52\frac{3}{4}$ x $40\frac{1}{4}$ x $25\frac{1}{4}$	372	551
3600	1972	67	200	Called the "Super Star." it has a tri-panelled glass grille in a spectrum of tangerine shades or is available in aquamarine shades. It introduced the Wurlitzer BO/AC coin accumulator. With a quick change of printed circuit cards you can change the money per play combination. It also has "Louver Controlled Light" in the titlestrip area.	$52\frac{1}{2}$ x $40\frac{1}{4}$ x $25\frac{1}{4}$	374	553
3610	1972	—	100	See 3600.	$52\frac{1}{2}$ x $40\frac{1}{4}$ x $25\frac{1}{4}$	371	553
3660	1972	—	160	See 3600.	$52\frac{1}{2}$ x $40\frac{1}{4}$ x $25\frac{1}{4}$	371	553
7500	1972	68	200	Called the "Cabaret."	$31\frac{1}{4}$ x 51 x 24	375	553
7500-A	1973	—	200	See 7500.	$31\frac{1}{4}$ x 51 x 24	375	556
7500-B	1973	—	200	See 7500.	$31\frac{1}{4}$ x 51 x 24	375	556
3700	1973	69	200	Called the "Americana."	$52\frac{1}{4}$ x $40\frac{1}{4}$ x $27\frac{7}{16}$	385	556
3710	1973	—	100	See 3700.	$52\frac{1}{4}$ x $40\frac{1}{4}$ x $27\frac{7}{16}$	383	556
3760	1973	—	160	See 3700.	$52\frac{1}{4}$ x $40\frac{1}{4}$ x $27\frac{7}{16}$	386	556
1050	1973	70	100	The "Nostaligia Model" It is a limited edition model. It uses 3710 components.	$57\frac{7}{8}$ x $36\frac{1}{4}$ x $28\frac{3}{4}$	365	556
3800	1974	71	200	Called the "Americana 3800." The last American-made Wurlitzer Jukebox model.	$52\frac{1}{4}$ x 40 x $27\frac{3}{4}$	357	556
3810	1974	—	100	See 3800.	$52\frac{1}{4}$ x 40 x $27\frac{3}{4}$	356	556
3860	1974	—	160	See 3800.	$52\frac{1}{4}$ x 40 x $27\frac{3}{4}$	358	556

North Tonawanda, New York

Hullhorst, Germany

Model	year of shipment	picture on page	number of selections	miscellaneous	dimensions (inches) H x W x D	weight/ kg.
Atlanta 3	1975	73	160		46.5 x 39.8 x 25.2	147kg.
Baltic	1975	76 upper	160		44.0 x 34.3 x 24.8	128kg.
Lyric	1975-80		100		40.0 x 32.7 x 23.8	108kg.
	1975	80 upper				
	1976	80 lower				
	1977	81				
	1978	82				
	1979-80	83				
Tarock	1975-84		100		32.0 x 42.1 x 22.6	123kg.
	1975-78	84				
	1979-81	85				
	1982-84	86				
X2	1976	87	160		52.7 x 39.8 x 25.2	153kg.
Baltic II	1976	76 lower	160		44.0 x 34.3 x 24.8	128 kg.
Cabaret	1976-78		160		32.9 x 52.7 x 24.0	170kg.
	1976	88				
	1977	89				
	1978	—				
X5	1977	90	160		52.7 x 39.8 x 25.2	148kg.
Niagara	1977	92	160		46.0 x 36.5 x 23.5	115kg.
Baltic 3	1977	77	160		44.0 x 34.3 x 24.8	128kg.
X7	1978	91	160		52.7 x 39.8 x 25.2	148kg.
Niagara 2	1978	93	160		46.0 x 36.5 x 23.5	115kg.
Baltic 4	1978	78	160		44.0 x 34.3 x 24.8	128kg.
Baltic 100	1978	79	100		44.0 x 34.3 x 24.8	128kg.
Cabarina	1978-83		160		32.9 x 43.3 x 24.0	165kg.
	1978	97				
	1979-81	98				
	1982-83	99				
X9	1979-80	100	160		52.7 x 39.8 x 25.2	148kg.
X9 electronic	1979	101	160	Microprocessor controlled. This means the traditional selector unit as well as the credit unit has been replaced by an electronic selection and credit computer (SCC).	52.7 x 39.8 x 25.2	148kg.
X200 electronic	1979-80	101	200		52.7 x 39.8 x 25.2	148kg.
Atlanta 4	1979	72	160		51.5 x 38.5 x 25.0	115kg.
Niagara 3	1979	94	160		46.0 x 36.5 x 23.5	115kg.

Model	year of shipment	picture on page	number of selections	miscellaneous	dimensions (inches) H x W x D	weight/ kg.
Atlanta 200 electronic	1980	74	200	It has a Play Stimulator: Plays automatically a record every 10-30 minutes (adjustable).	51.5 x 38.5 x 25.0	143kg.
Atlanta 160	1980	72	160		51.5 x 38.5 x 25.0	143kg.
Carillon	1980	102*	160	Panels available in Regular and 3-D. *On page 102, the upper machine is Regular and the lower machine is 3-D.	46.0 x 32.5 x 23.5	127kg.
Atlanta 160	1981	75	160	SHURE magnetic pick-up. Electronic coin counter & electronic service checks.	52.7 x 39.8 x 25.2	148kg.
Atlanta 200	1981	75	200		52.7 x 39.8 x 25.2	148kg.
Silhouette	1981	103*	160	Panels available in Regular and 3-D. *On page 103, the upper machine is Regular and the lower machine is 3-D.	47.0 x 32.5 x 23.5	118kg.
Niagara 4	1981	95	160		46.0 x 36.5 x 23.5	110kg.
Estrella	1982	104	200		53.3 x 40.0 x 25.2	159kg.
Niagara 5	1982	96	160		46.0 x 36.5 x 23.5	122kg.
Caravelle	1983-84	105	200		53.3 x 40.0 x 25.2	159kg.
Barcarole	1983	—	200	Same as Caravelle, different panel.	53.3 x 40.0 x 25.2	159kg.
Fuego	1983-84	106	160		46.0 x 36.5 x 23.5	122kg.
Tele-Disc	1983-84	107	160		— — —	—
SL 700	1984	108	160	200 watts total music power. Model SL 700-A with additional continuous pulsating light-sound synchronized during record play.	54.9 x 38.8 x 25.6	153kg
Diana	1984	109	160		47.0 x 32.5 x 23.5	120kg.

THE COMMENCING SERIAL NUMBERS FOR THE MODELS ARE:

Year	Model	Serial number	
1975	Atlanta 3D	1418	7941
	Baltic	1420	0001
	Lyric 3D	1419	8093
	Tarock	1419	8101
1976	Lyric	5519	0001
	Tarock	5519	0001
	Baltic II	1519	0942
	Cabaret	1505	0299
	X-2	1509	0968
1977	Lyric	5608	3326
	Tarock	5619	1001
	Cabaret	5619	0001
	X-5	1619	2841
	Niagara	1619	2880
	Baltic	5619	3434
1978	All models	5719	0001
1979	All models	5819	0001
1980	All models	5920	0001
1981	All models	6010	0001
1982	All models	6109	2855
1983	All models	6209	5073

WILCOX
"AMPLIPHONE"
MULTIPLE SELECTION

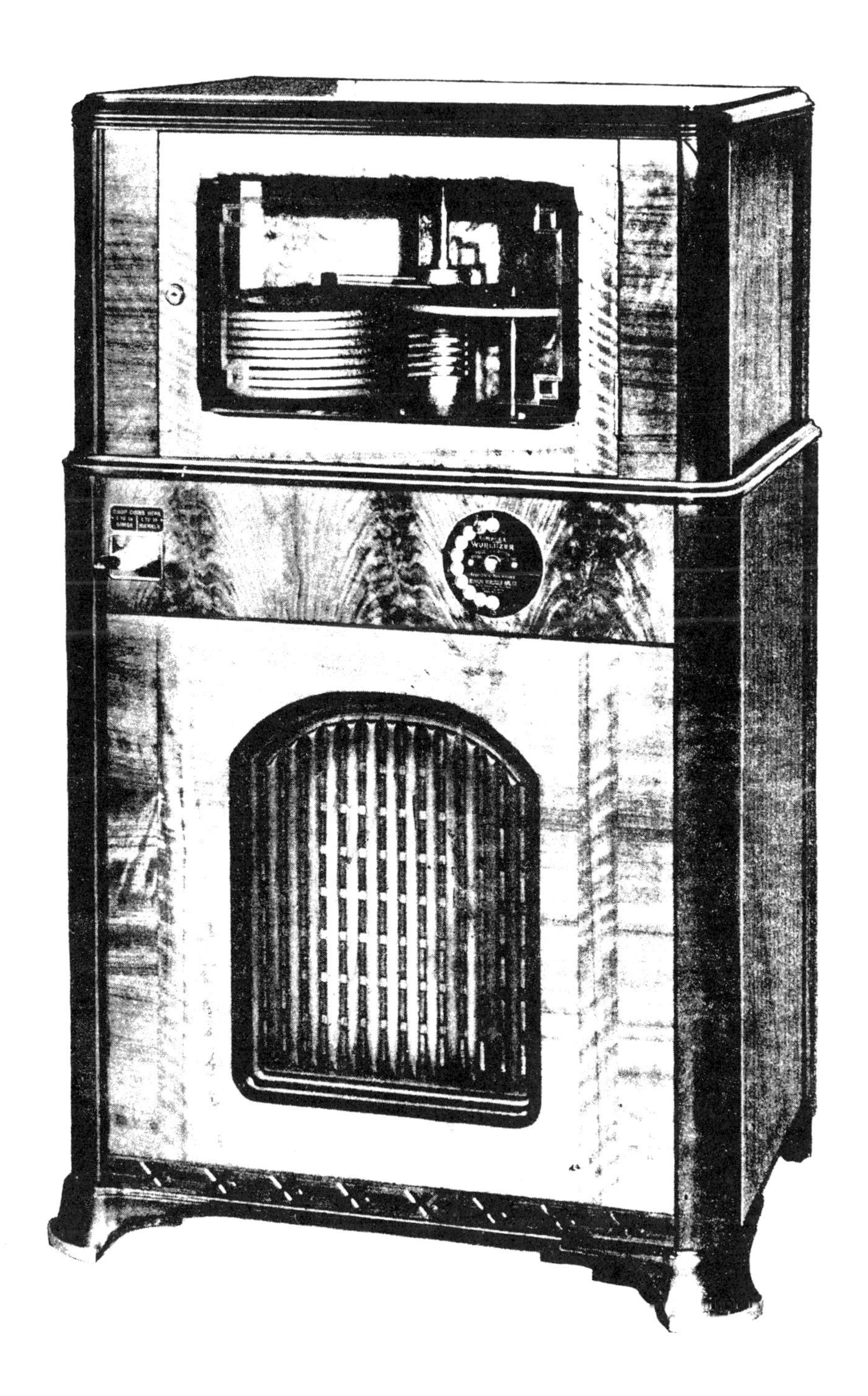

WURLITZER MODEL P-20

MODEL P-12 SIMPLEX

WURLITZER

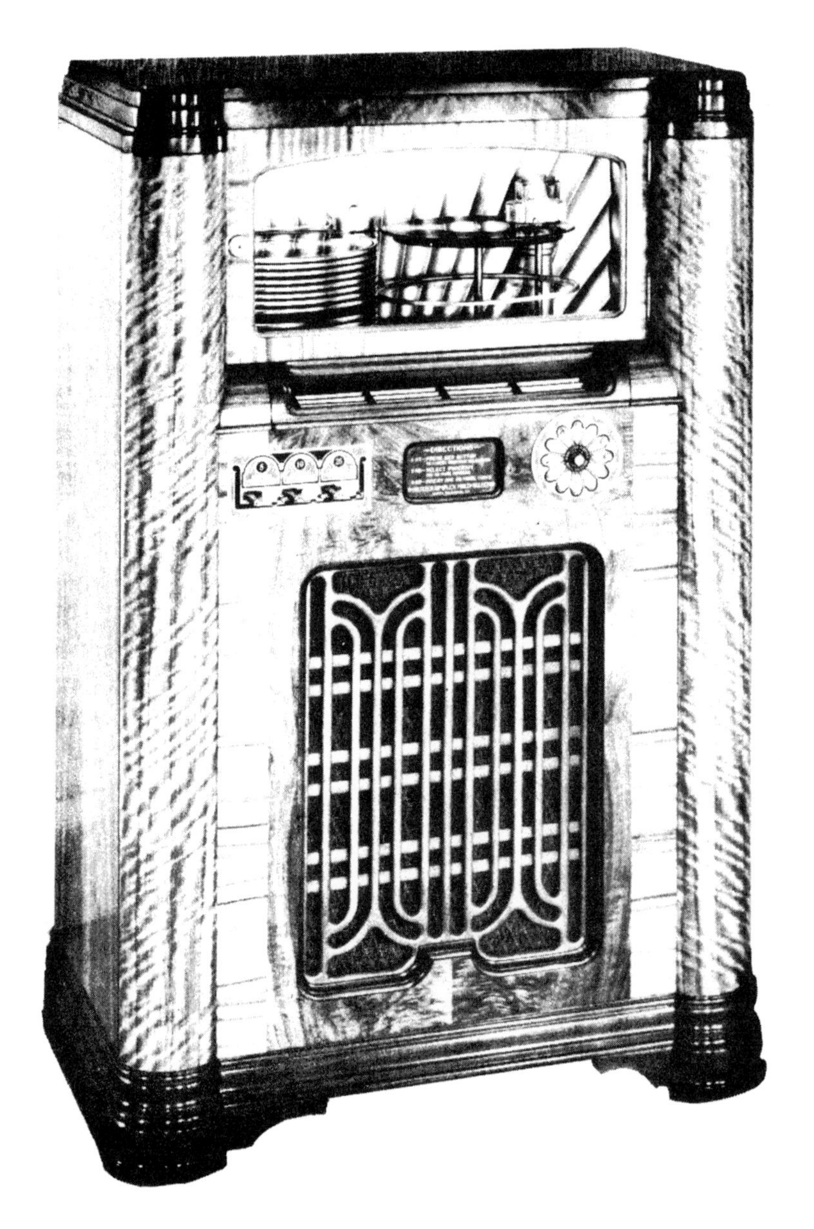

MODEL 412 SIMPLEX

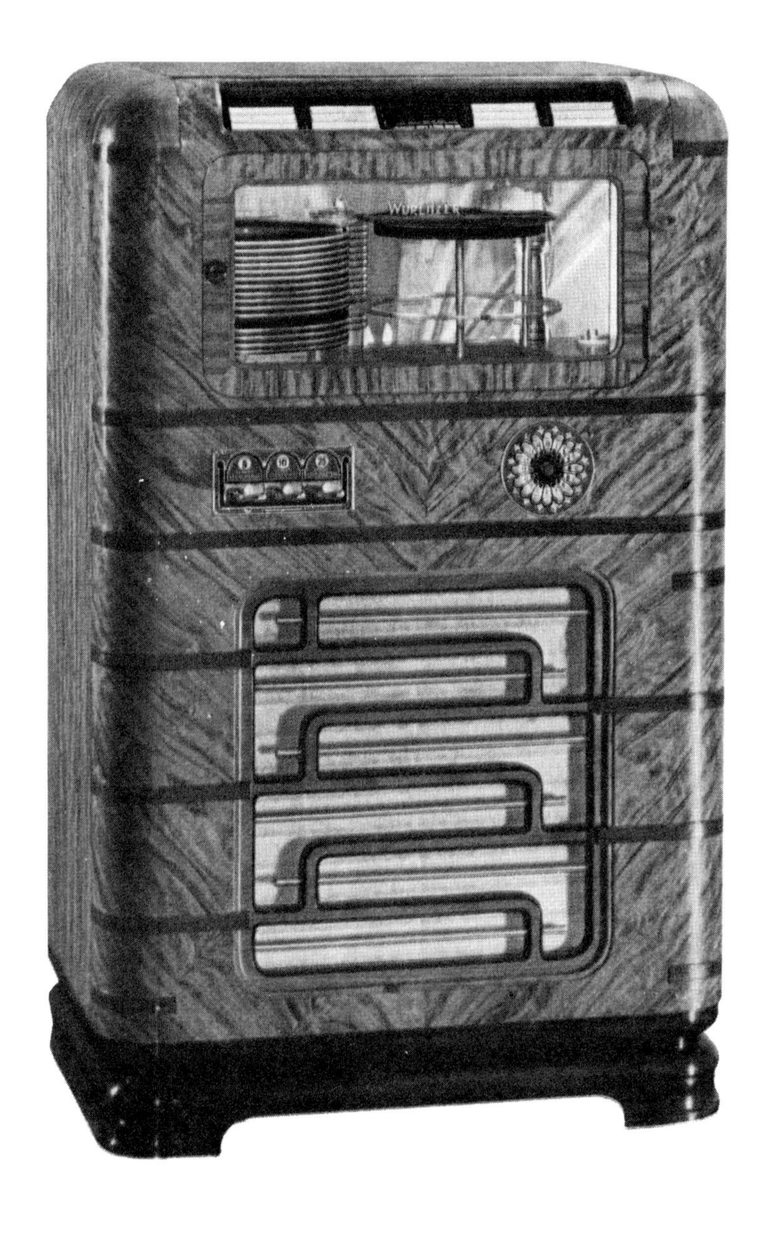

WURLITZER

WURLITZER

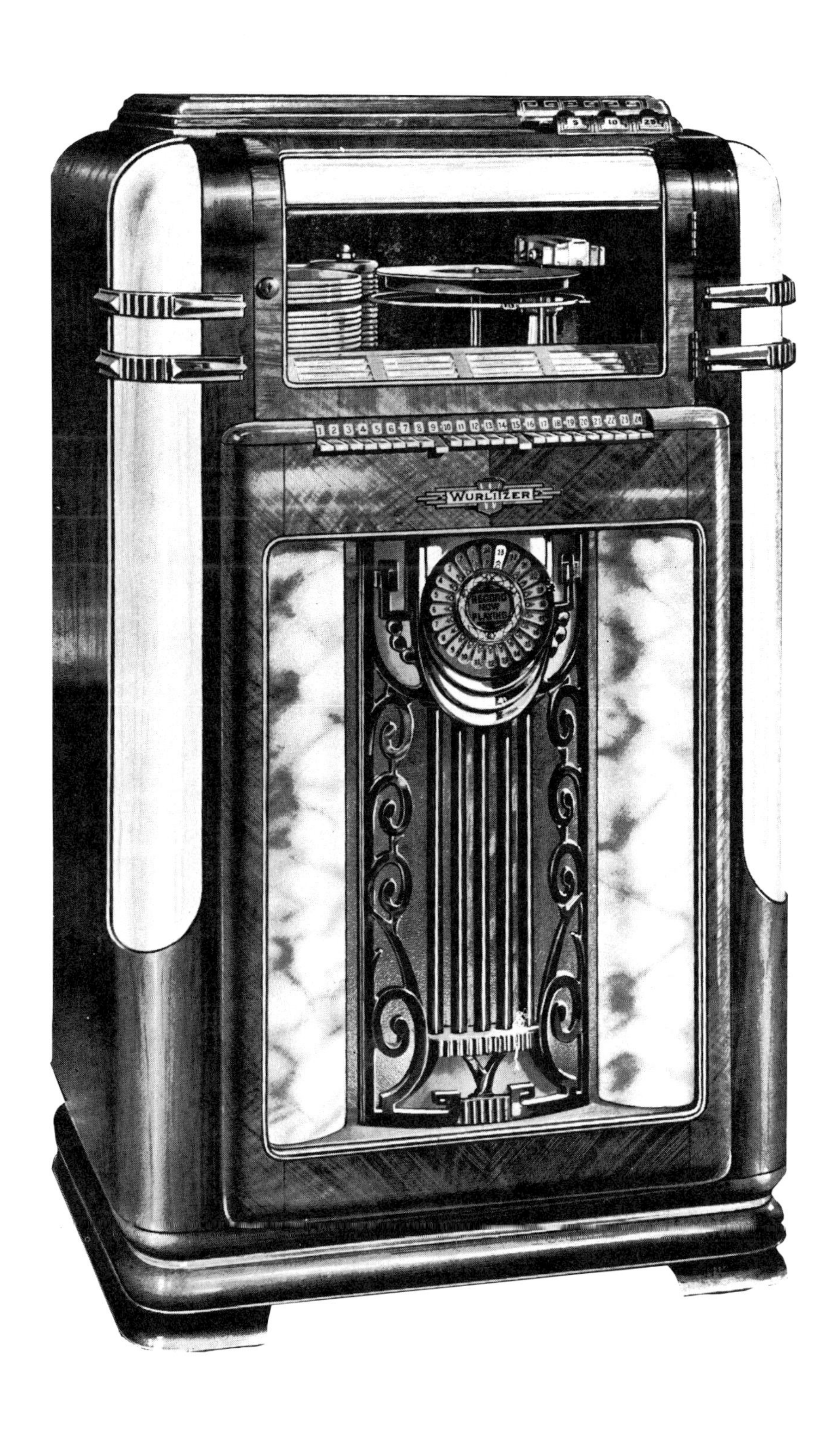
WURLITZER
RECORD NOW PLAYING

WURLITZER MODEL G-500

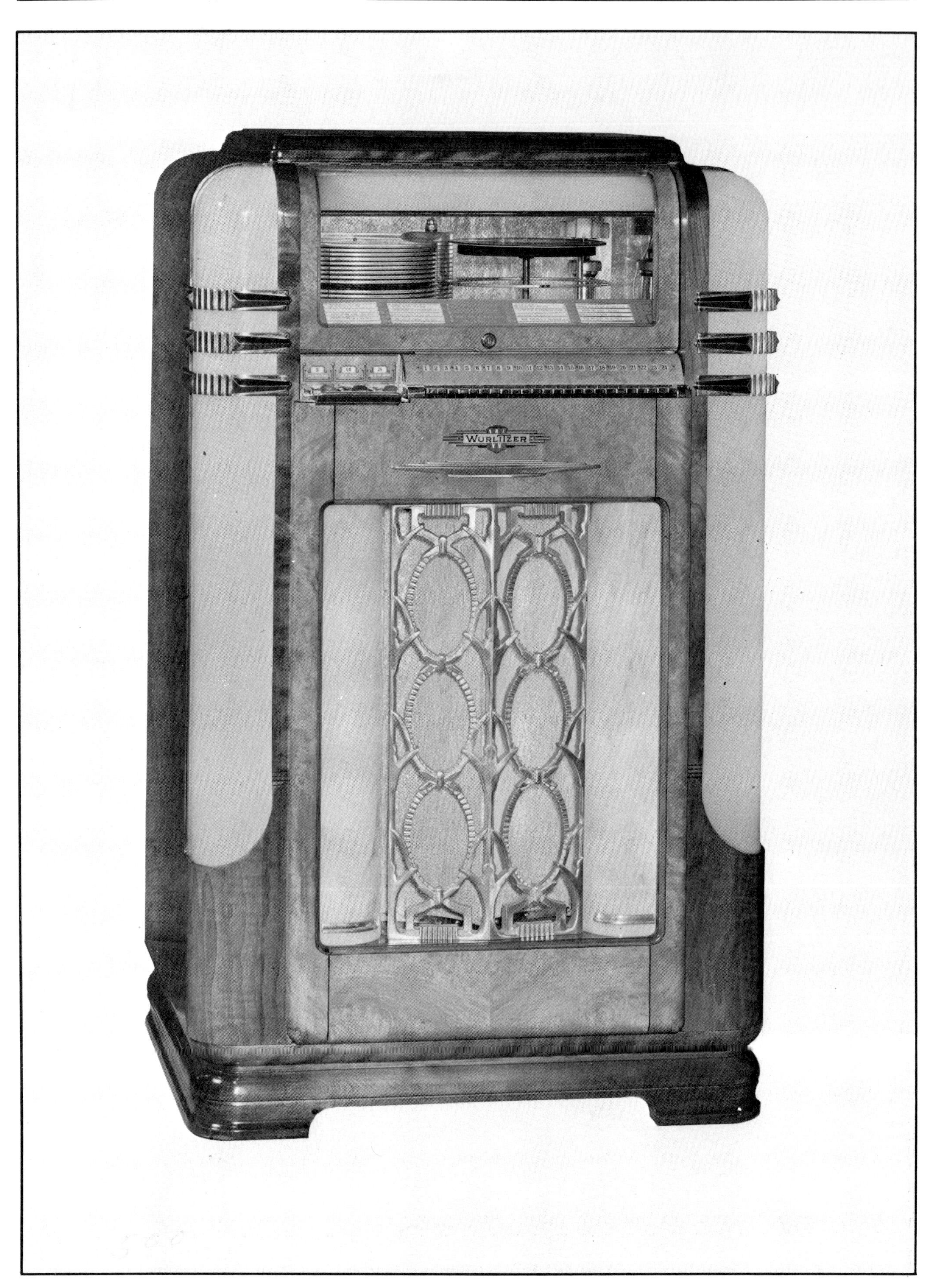

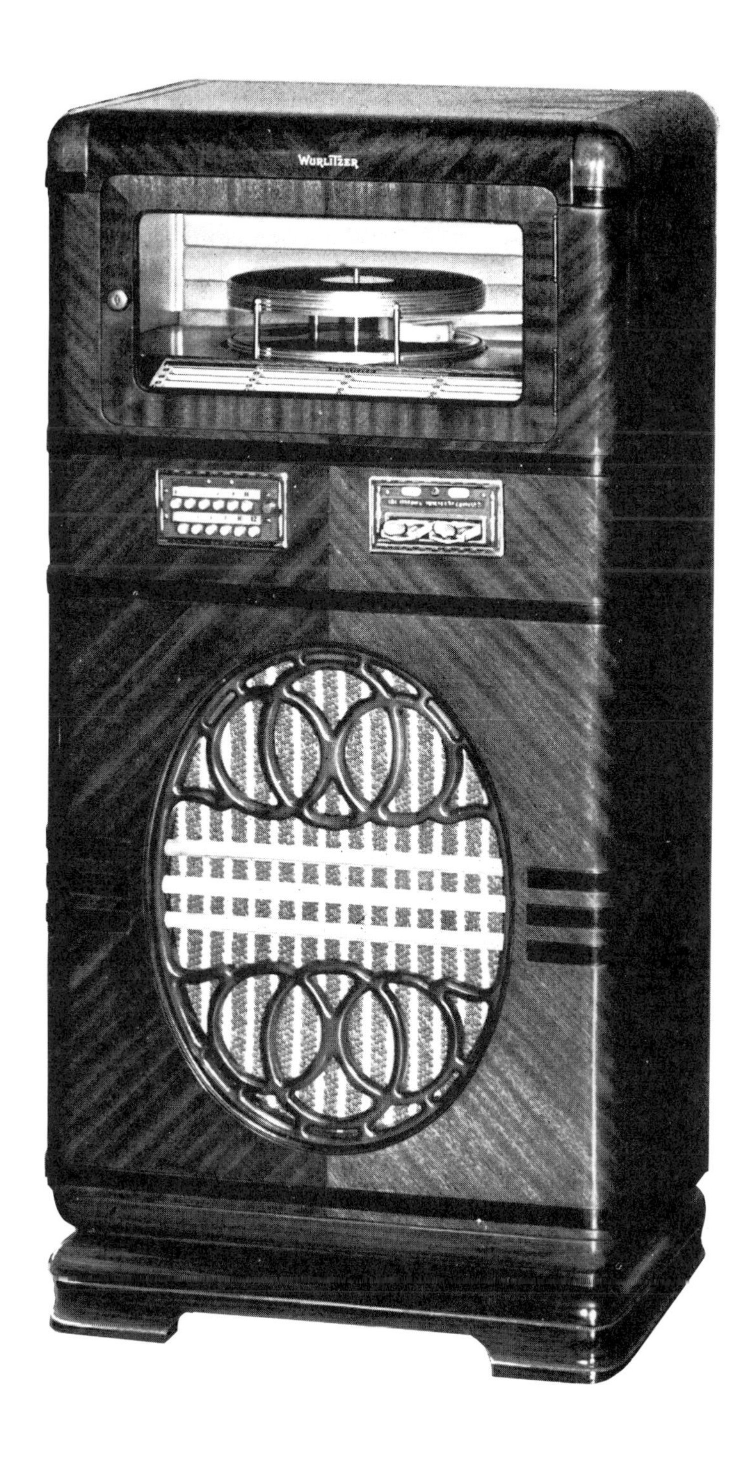
WURLITZER

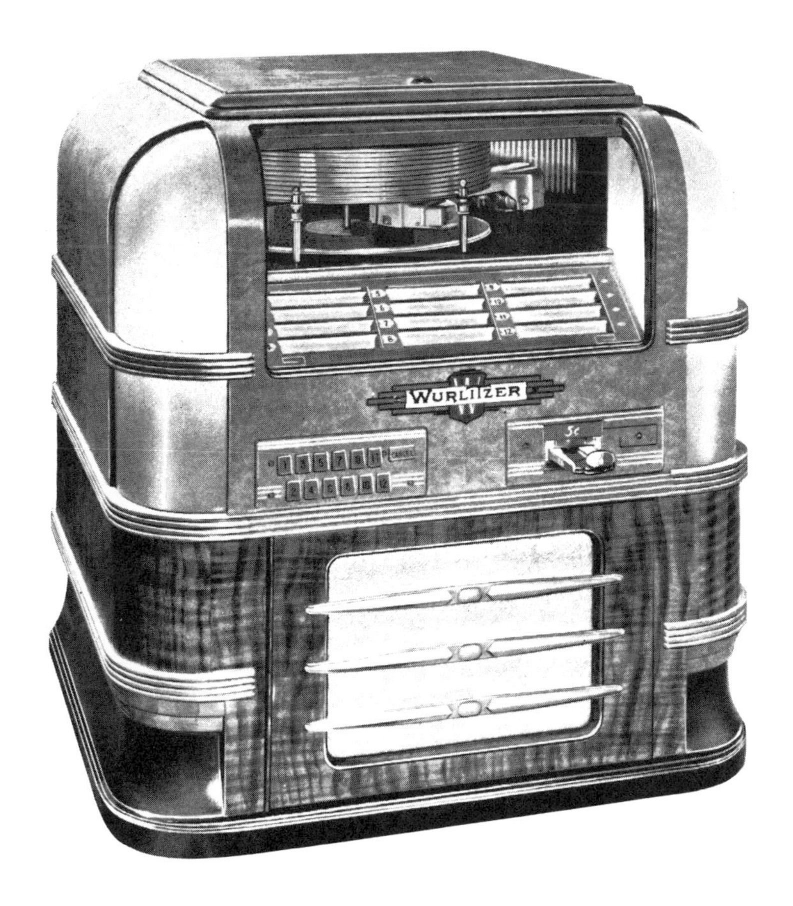
WURLITZER

WURLITZER
WURLITZER

WURLITZER
WURLITZER

MECHANICAL RECORD SELECTOR
HI SPEED SERVICE SET UP
MOTO DRIVE COIN SWITCH
MAGNETIC COIN SELECTOR
TRUE TRACKING TONE ARM
STEEL REINFORCED CABINETS
INSTANT SET-BACK PLAY METER
WURLITZER
WURLITZER

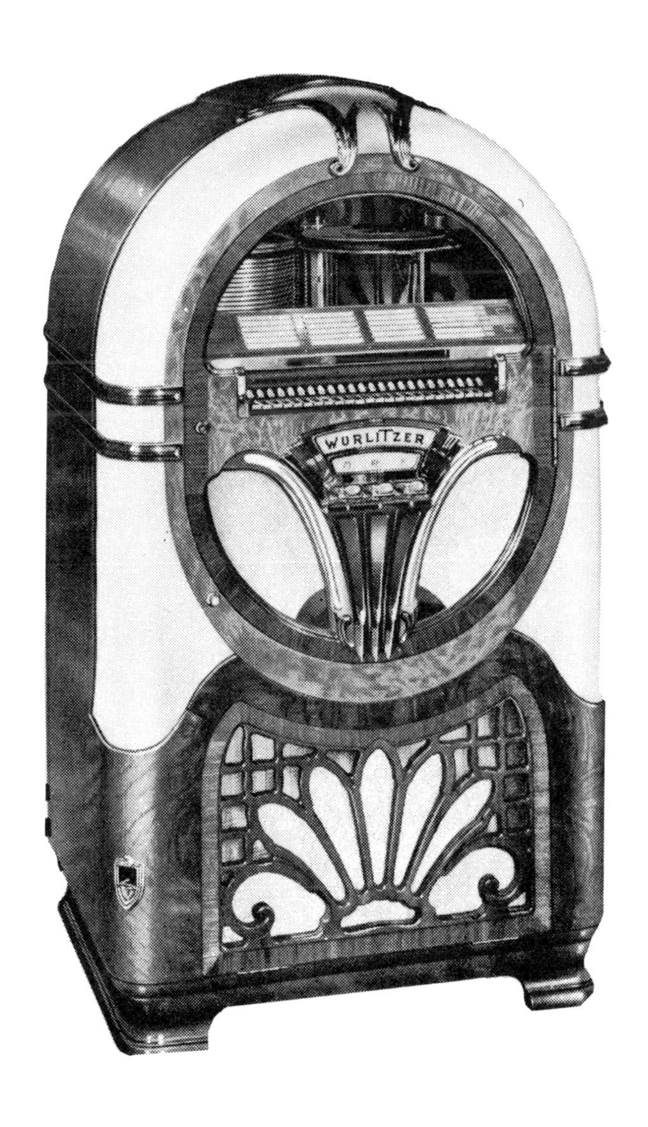
WURLITZER

The WURLITZER
Colonial
MODEL 780 for 1941
WURLITZER

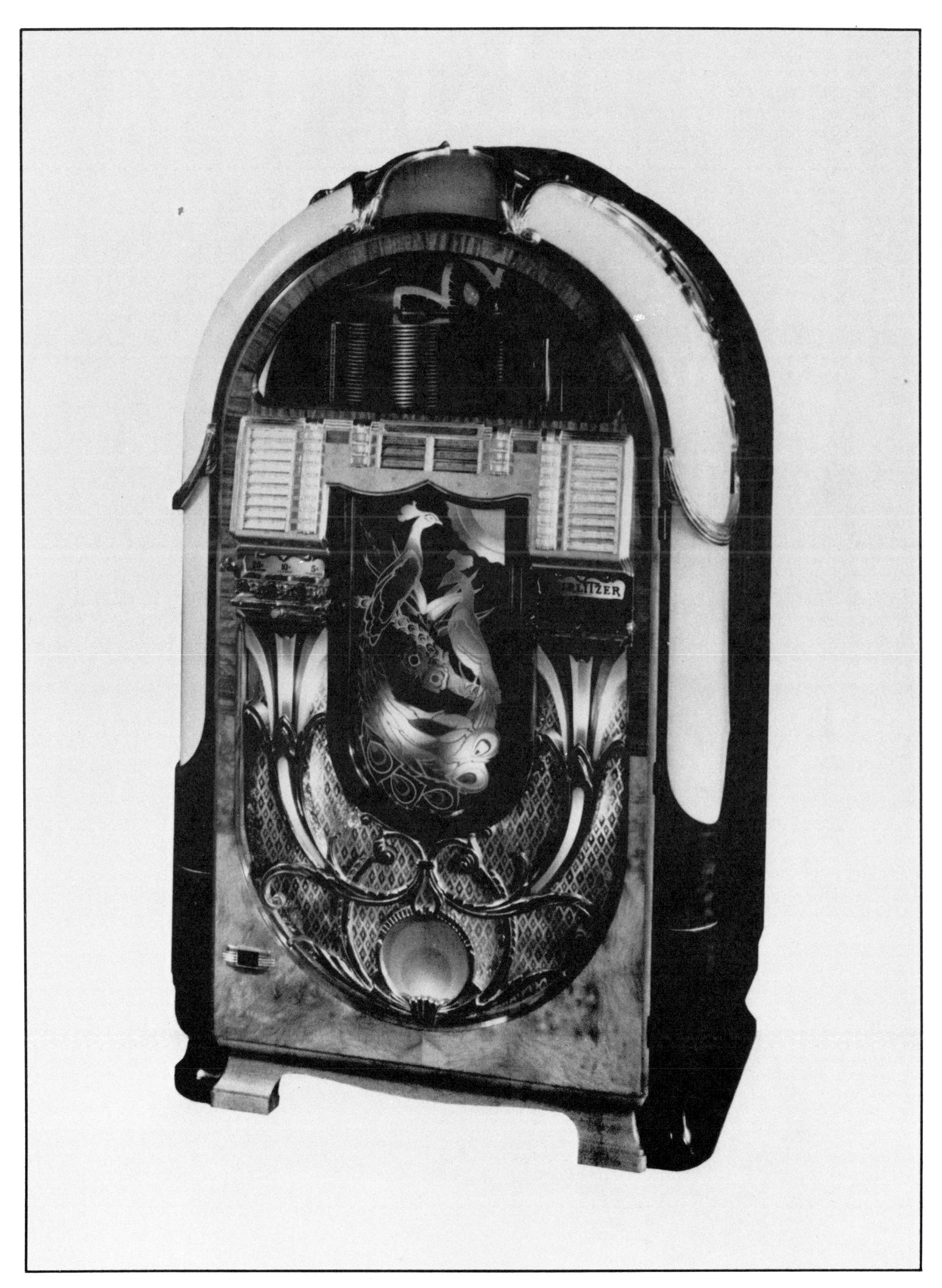
WURLITZER

WURLITZER MODEL 950

WURLITZER

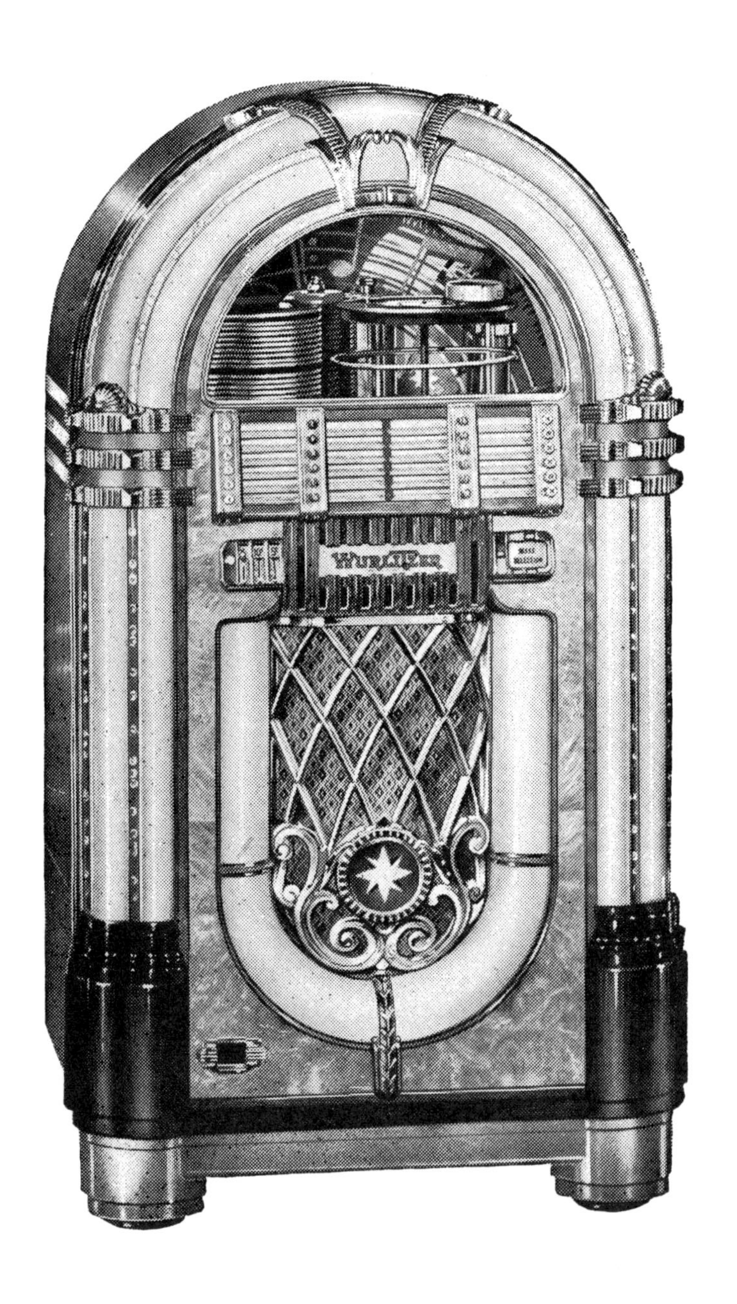
WURLITZER

WURLITZER

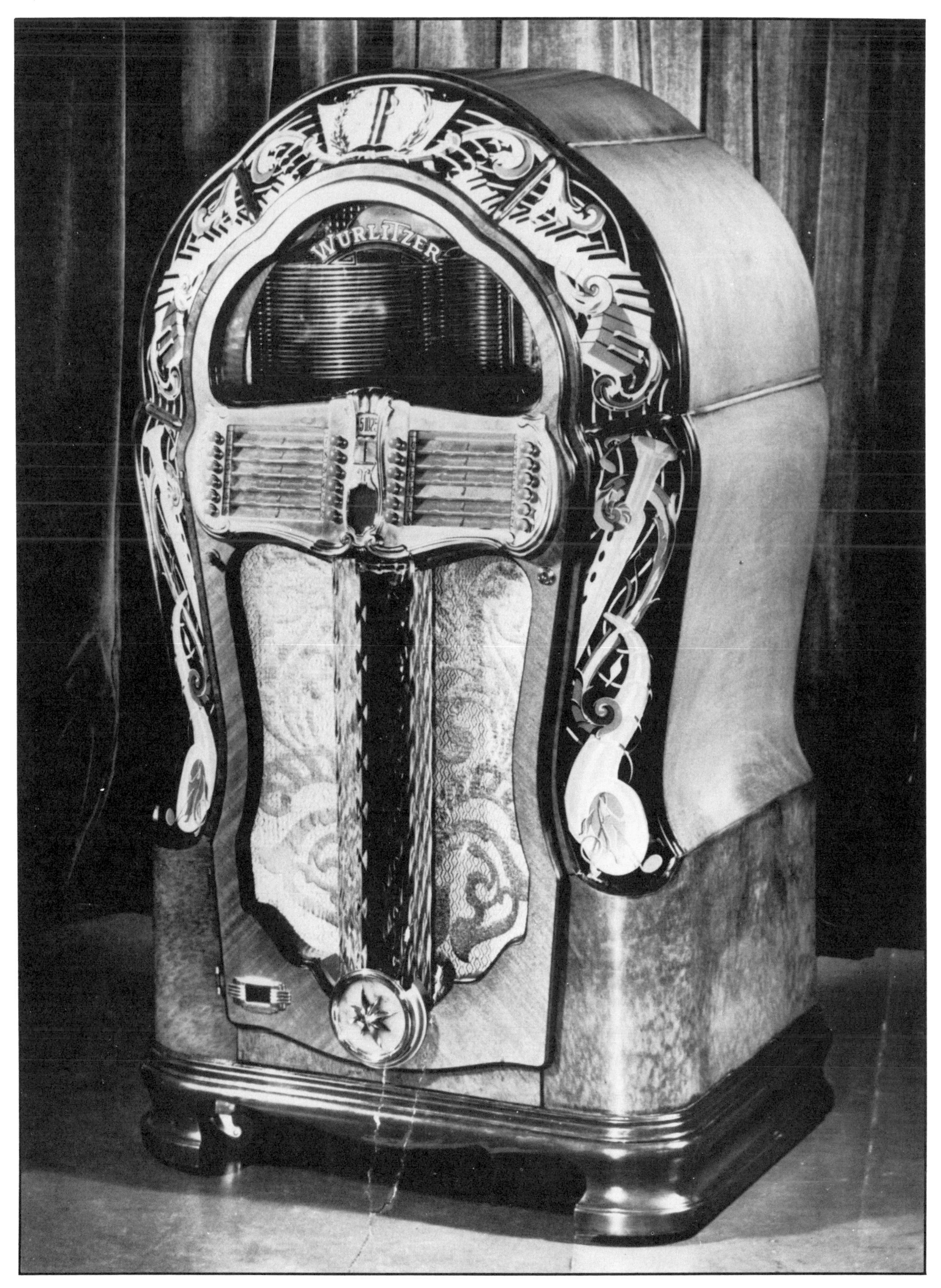
WURLITZER

WURLITZER
POPULAR
WALTZES
FOLK
CLASSICAL
WESTERN
POLKA

WURLITZER

WURLITZER
WURLITZER
POPULAR AND CURRENT HITS
CLASSICAL AND OLD FAVORITES
POLKAS AND SPECIALTIES
PRESS
A
B
C
D

WURLITZER MODEL 1550A

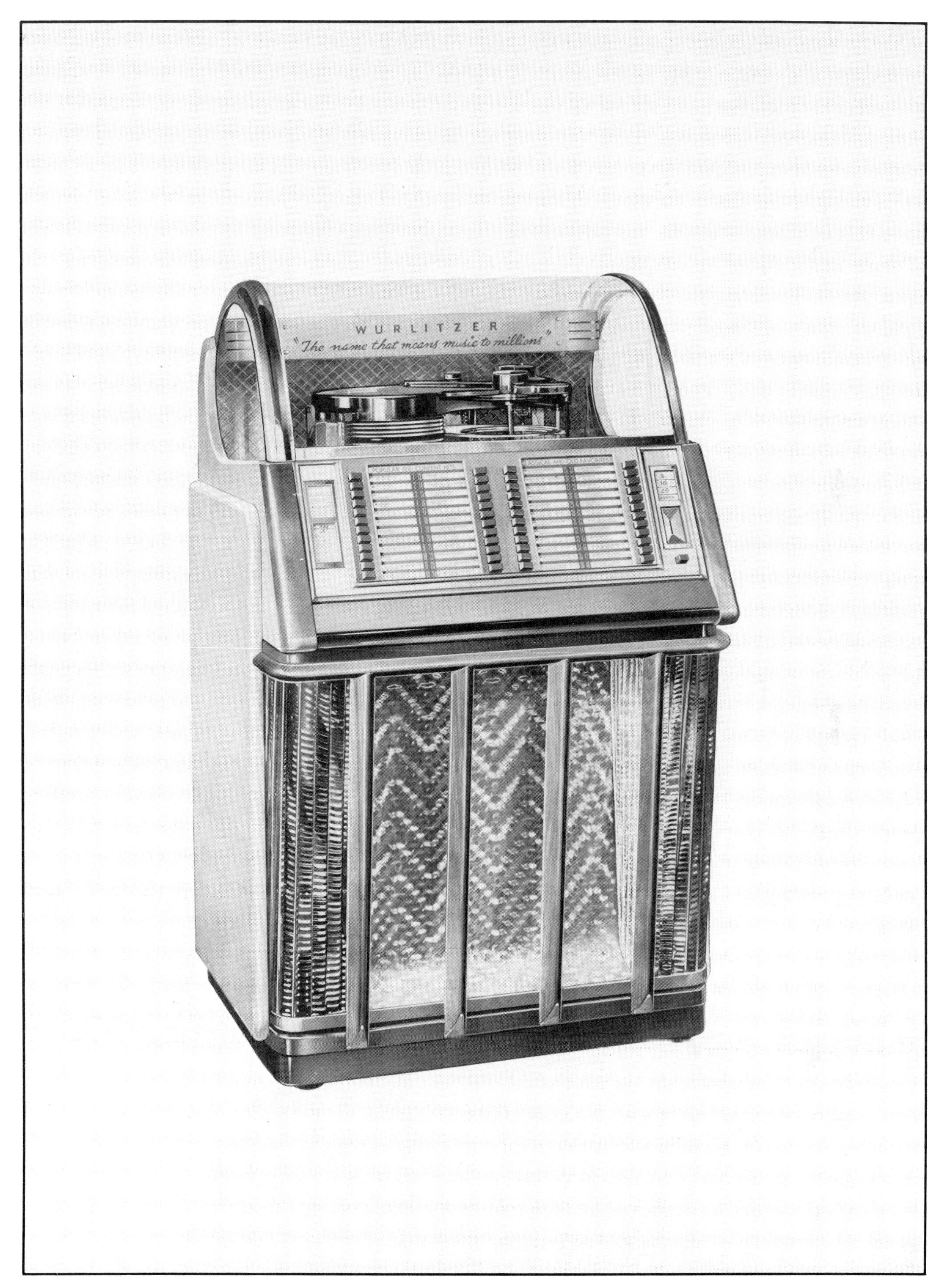
WURLITZER
"The name that means music to millions"

Model 1600 AF

THE SENSATIONAL NEW *Wurlitzer*

CAROUSEL RECORD CHANGER

Simplest Changer Ever Offered on a Multi-Selection Phonograph

The Carousel Record Changer utilizes one tone arm, one needle and one turntable direction, yet it plays both sides of 52 seven-inch 45 RPM records! Records are not turned over, not picked up by any clamping device. They are gently raised by one of two arms mounted on either side of the circular record holder . . . engaged by a self-centering metal chuck, secured into position by three metal fingers and played vertically. Record-now-playing indicator rises from slot in chassis shelf either side of record player. The turntable is driven by a combination of belt and gears for noiseless operation. The needle is brushed before and after each record is played. The entire mechanism is easily removable and will stand unsupported on its base for adjustment or service. Composed of four major assemblies, the Carousel Changer may be easily disassembled as illustrated here.

Here's how it works

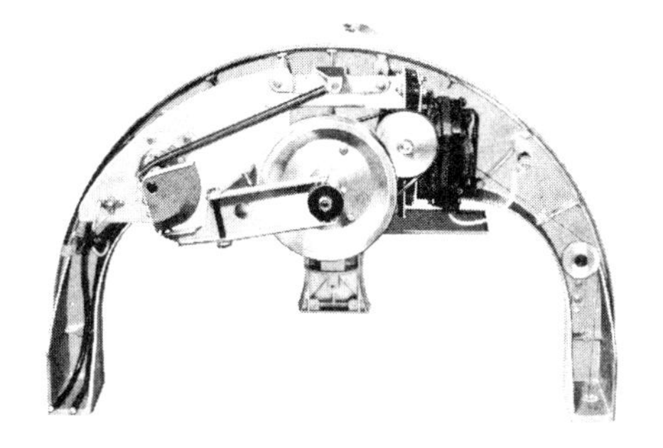

Semi-circular arch casting houses turntable motor, serves as a mount for tone arm and actuating mechanism. Turntable is flywheel balanced to assure accurate RPM.

EACH RECORD HAS ITS OWN PLAY-METER REGISTERING UP TO 60 PLAYS

The record lift mechanism is located directly below the record carrier. Consisting of a single cam and two clutches, which operate the record lifting arms and the tone arm position, this mechanism is actuated by a single reverse rotation direct current motor.

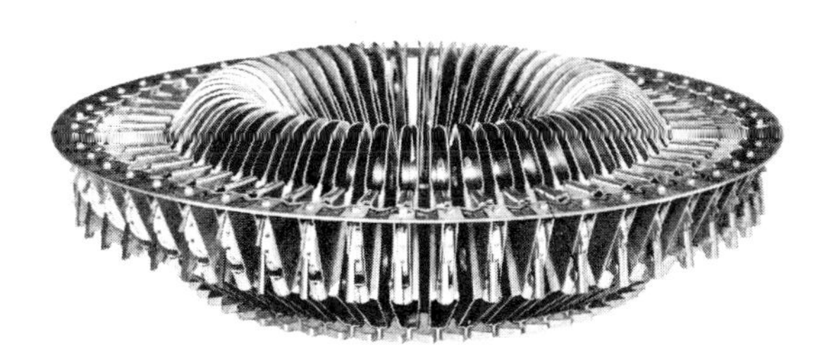

Carousel record carrier always revolves clockwise. Each of 52 sections holds a record and has its own Playmeter. Entire carrier mounts on the largest star wheel ever used on a juke box assuring accurate selection. Record holding device has disengagement switch enabling serviceman to shut off current and operating parts. The Carousel then free-wheels for loading or record changing.

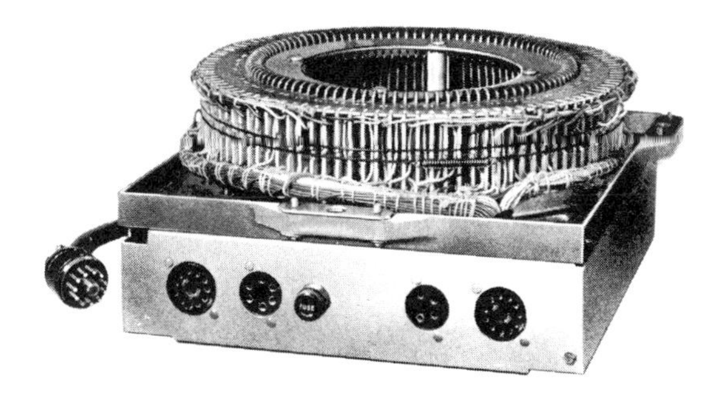

Suspended horizontally below the record lift mechanism is the selector drum and junction box. This selector unit completes the simplest mechanism ever offered on a multi-selection phonograph.

WURLITZER MODEL 1700HF

Wurlitzer
A B C D

WURLITZER MODEL 1900

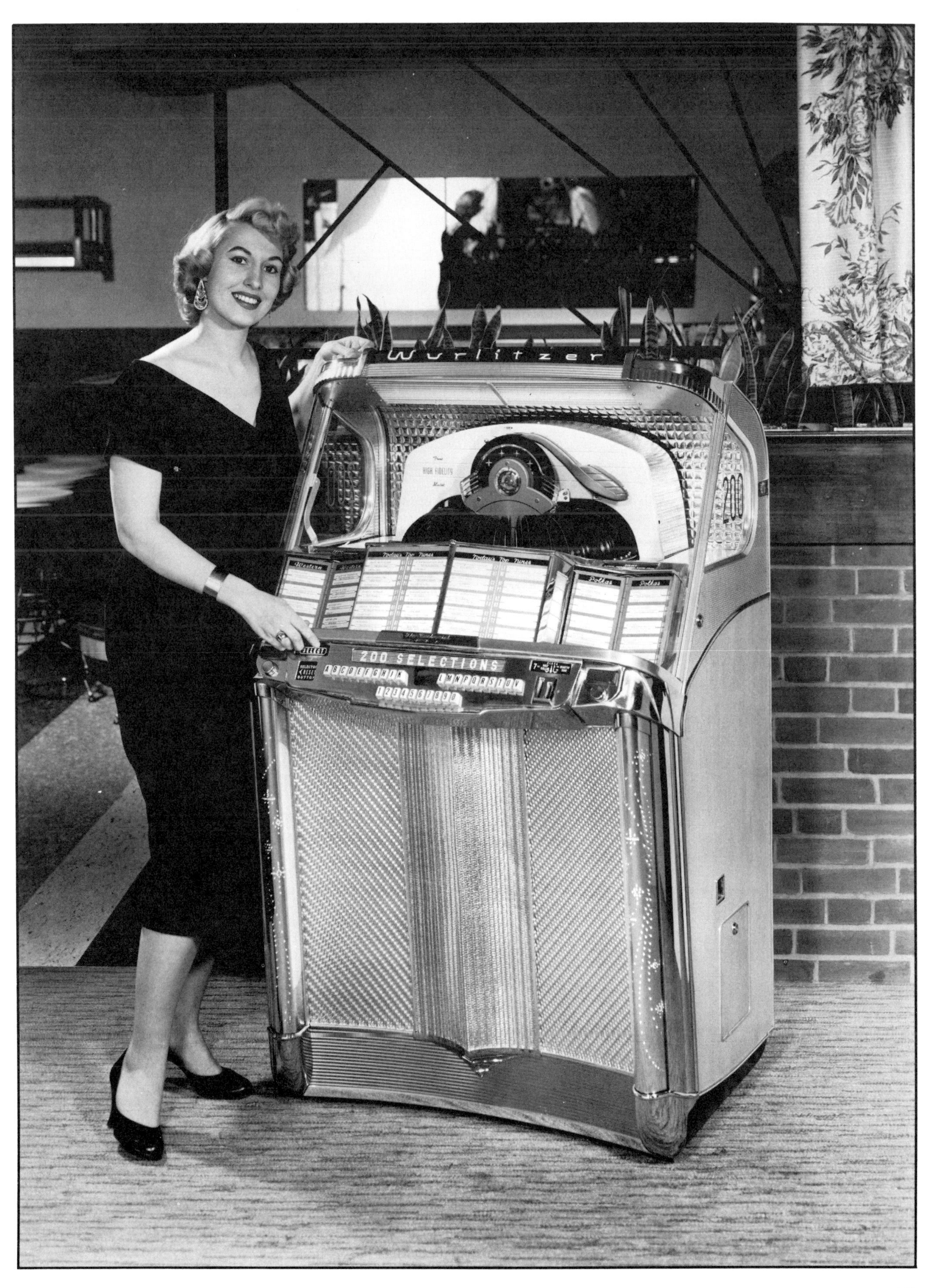
Wurlitzer
200 SELECTIONS
200

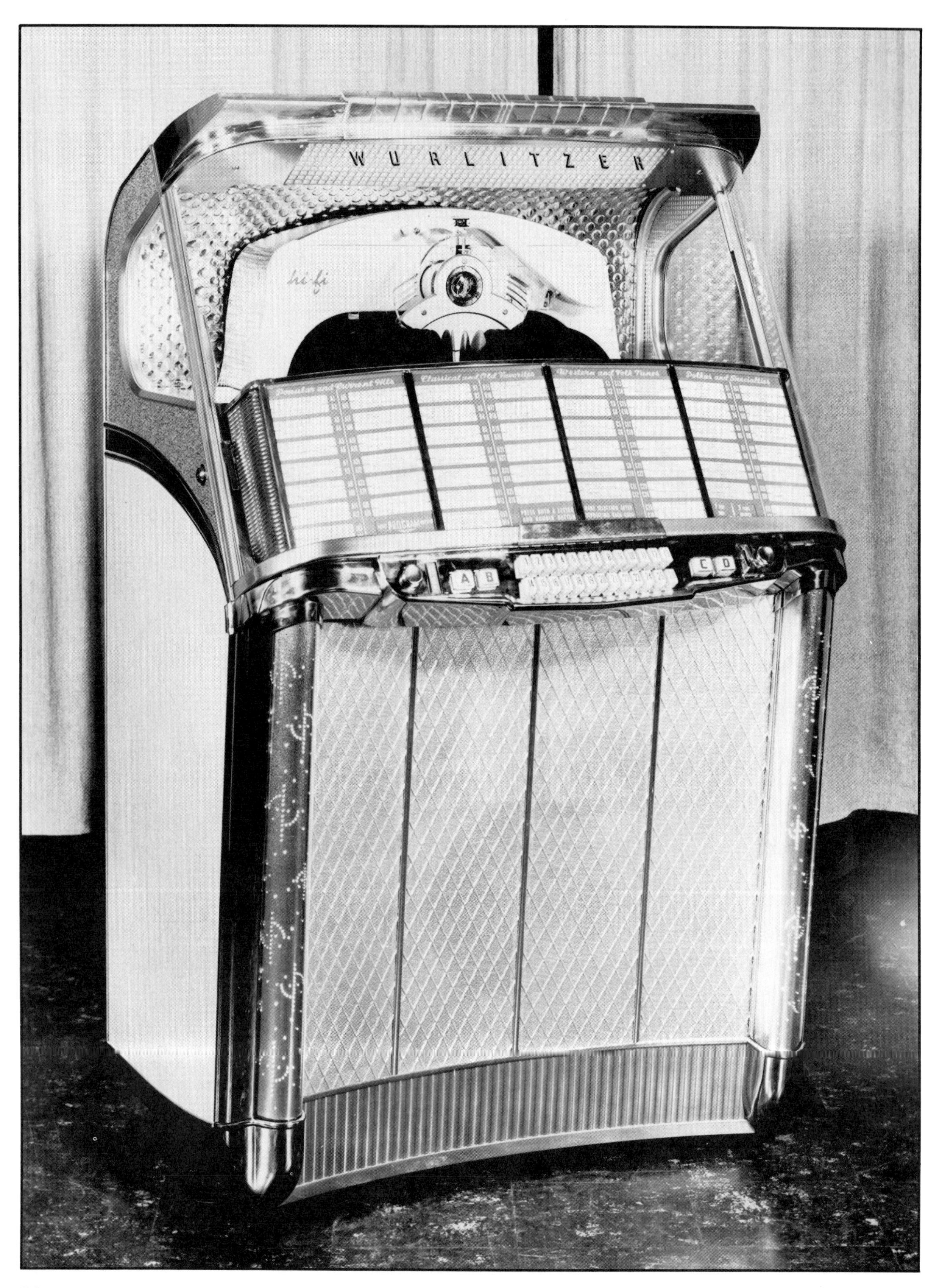
WURLITZER
hi-fi
Popular and Current Hits
Classical and Old Favorites
Western and Folk Tunes
Polkas and Specialties
A B
C D

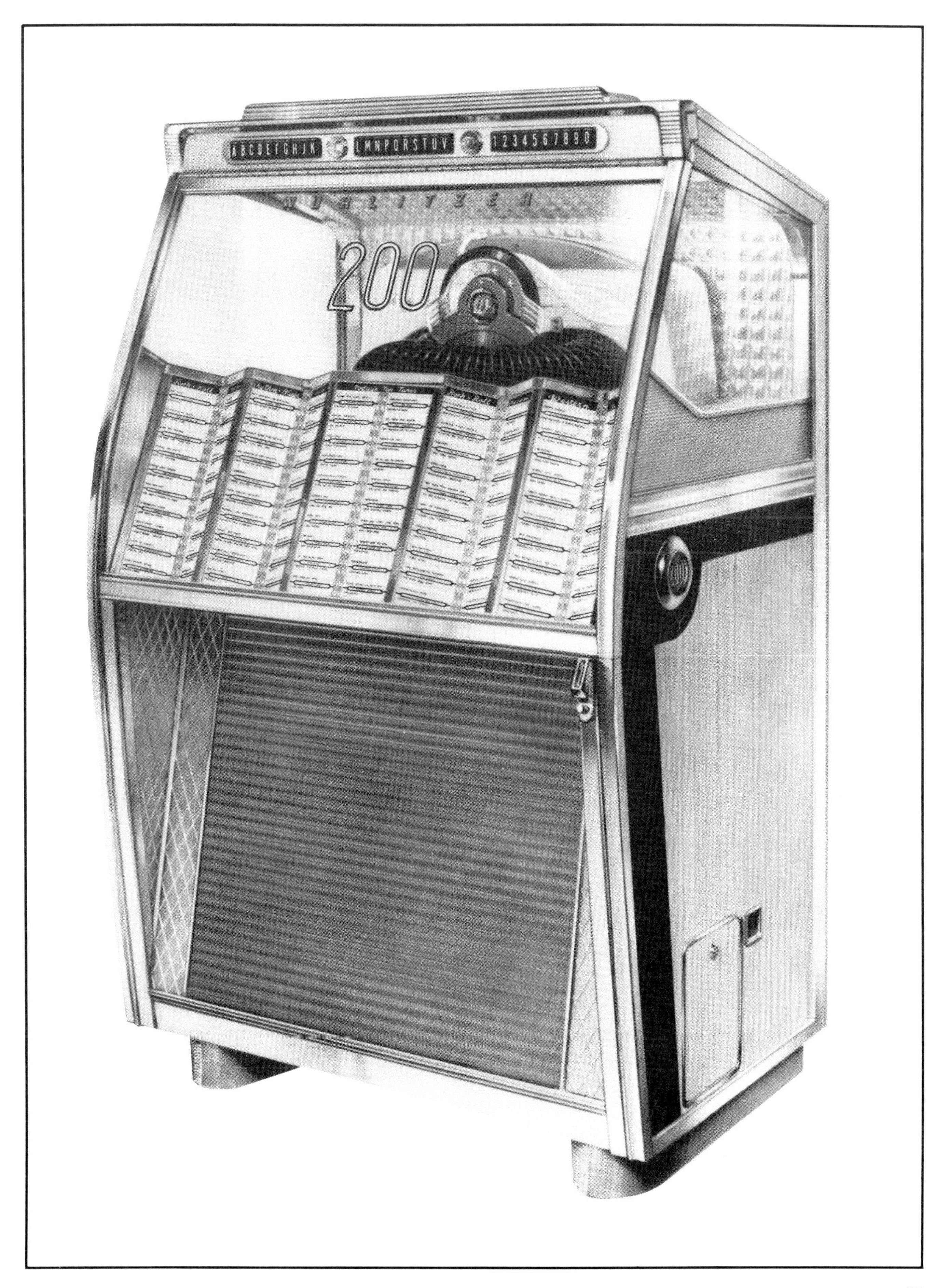
ABCDEFGHJK
LMNPQRSTUV
1234567890
WURLITZER
200

Wurlitzer

WURLITZER
HI-FIDELITY

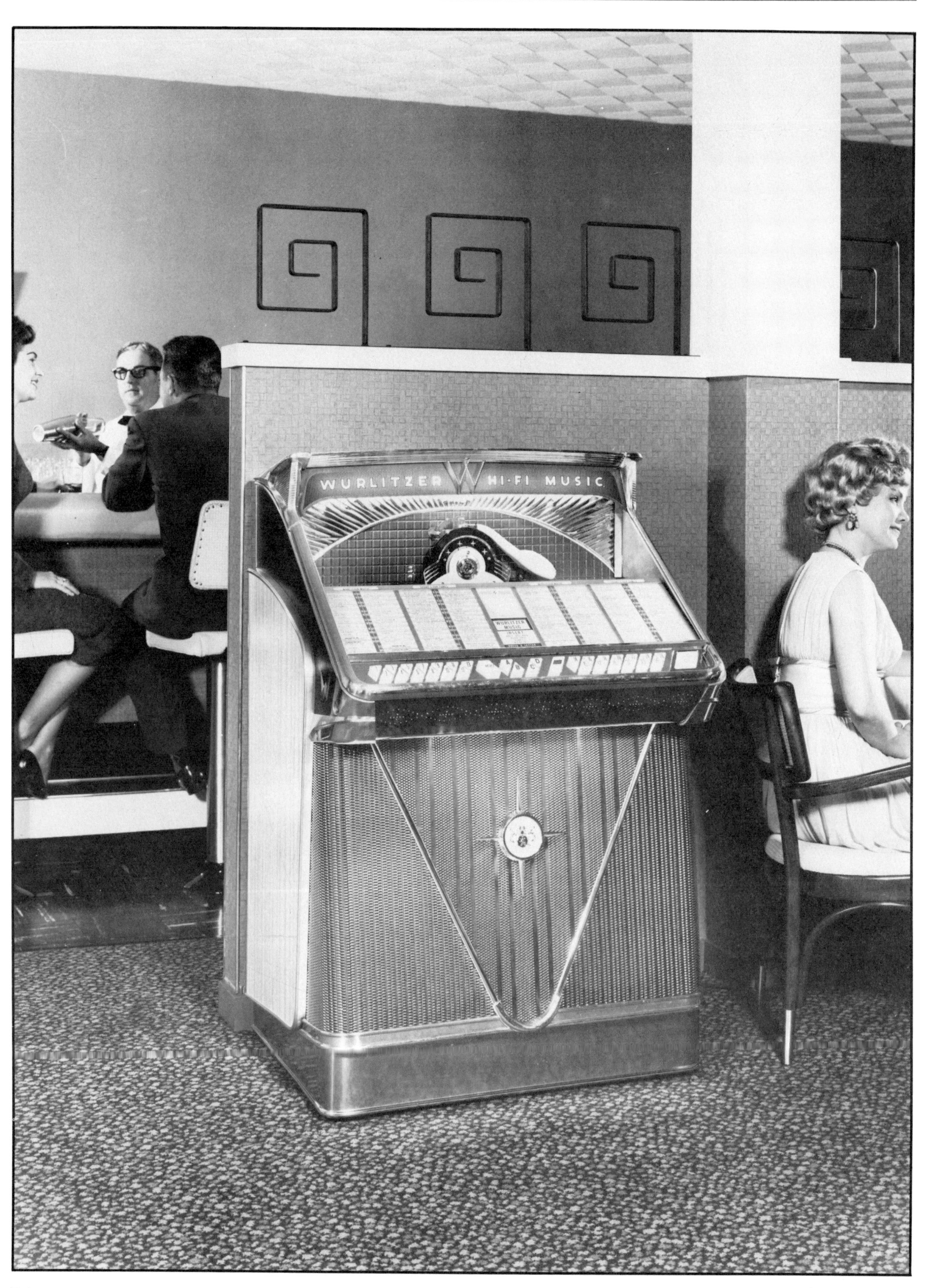
WURLITZER
HI-FI MUSIC

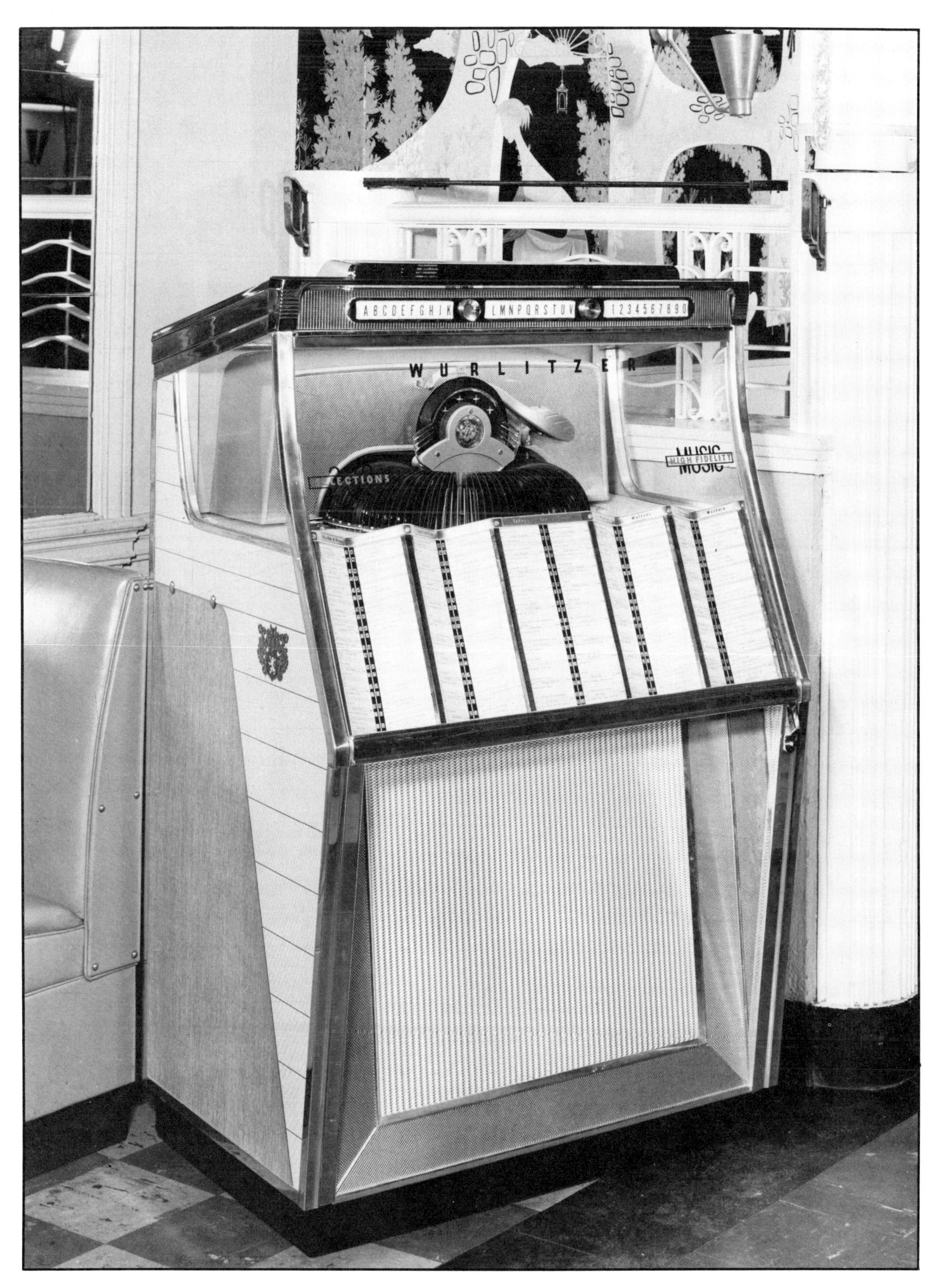
ABCDEFGHJK
LMNPQRSTUV
1234567890
WURLITZER
HIGH FIDELITY
MUSIC

Stereophonic Music
WURLITZER

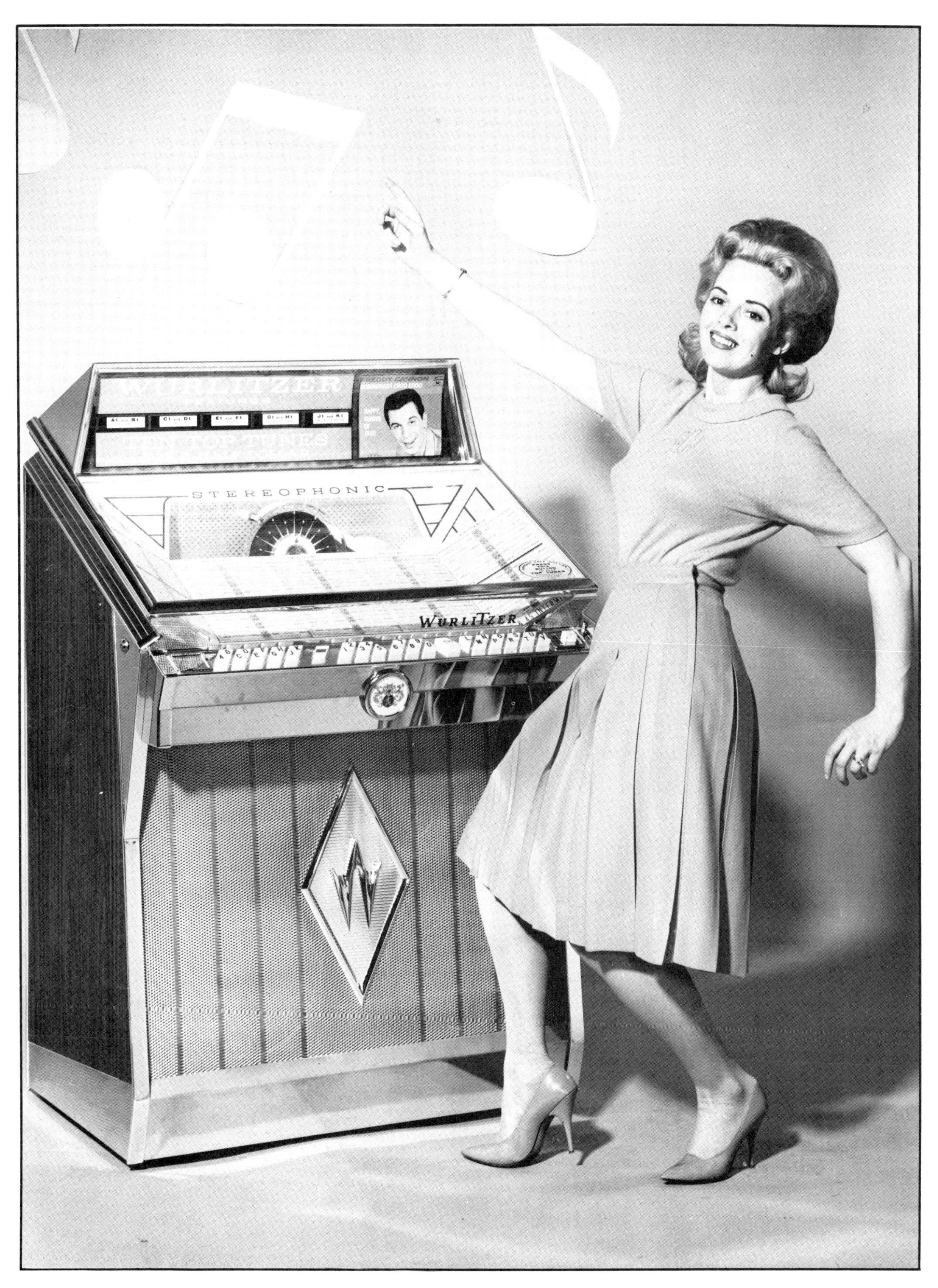
WURLITZER
FREDDY CANNON
STEREOPHONIC
WURLITZER

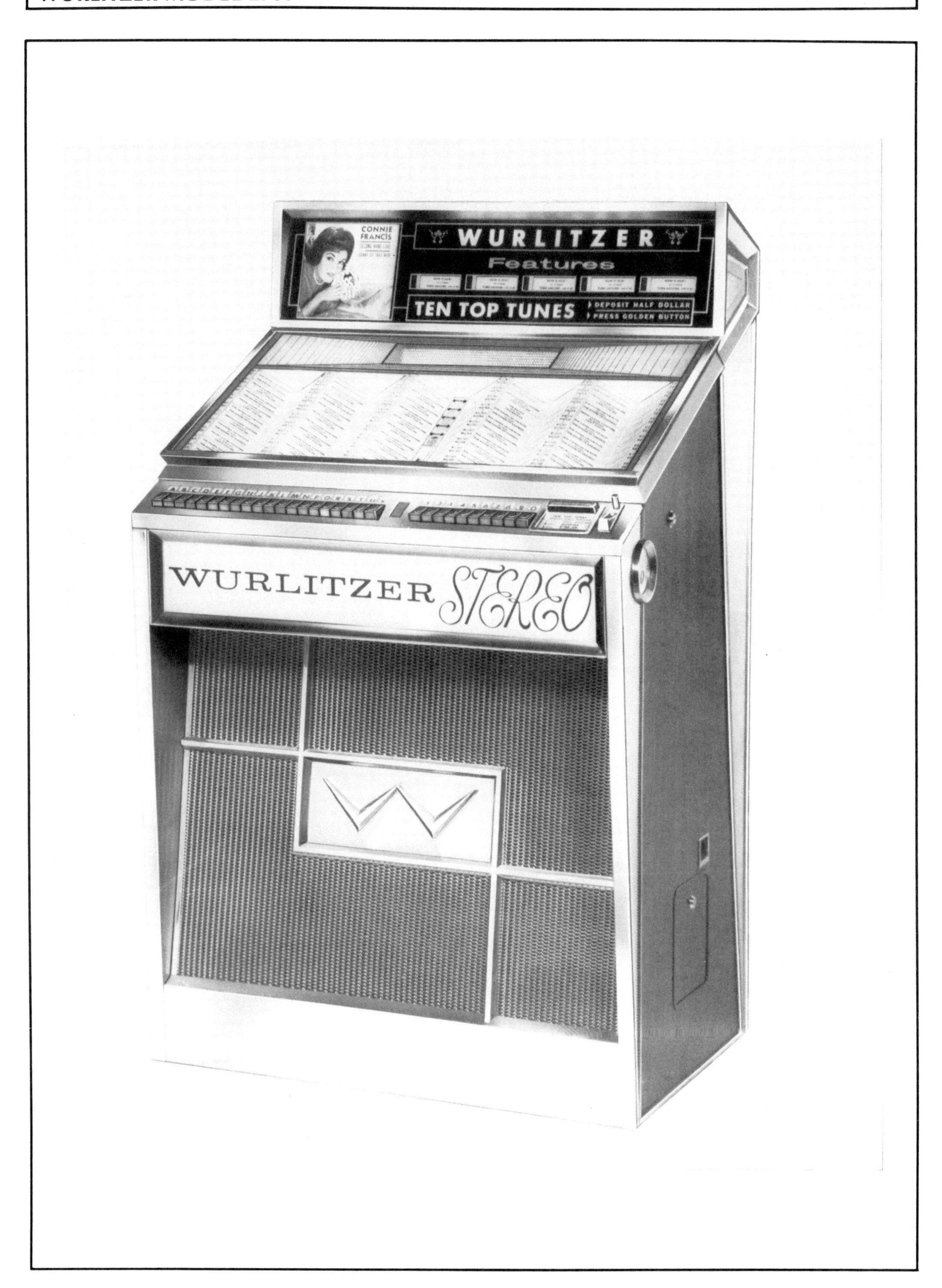
CONNIE FRANCIS
WURLITZER
Features
TEN TOP TUNES
DEPOSIT HALF DOLLAR
PRESS GOLDEN BUTTON
WURLITZER STEREO

LA BOHEMIA TAVERN
stereo ... by WURLITZER

WURLITZER MODEL 2900

WURLITZER
STEREO MUSIC CENTER
WURLITZER

Americana
WURLITZER

SOLID STATE STEREO
AMERICANA II
WURLITZER

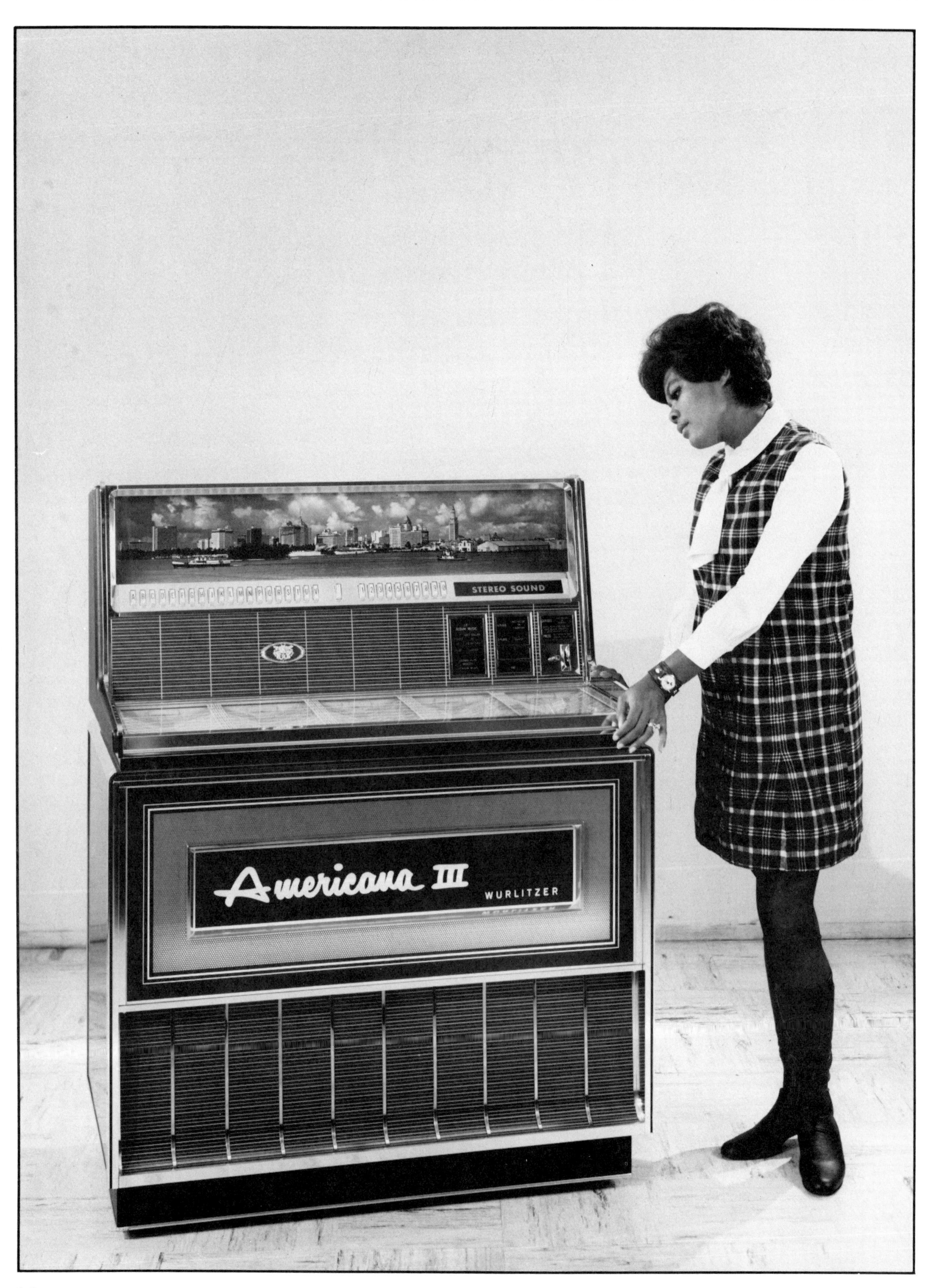
STEREO SOUND
Americana III
WURLITZER

STATESMAN
BY WURLITZER

Music for Millions
A B C D E F G H J K L M N P Q R S T U V
1 2 3 4 5 6 7 8 9 0
ZODIAC
WURLITZER

WURLITZER

WURLITZER
Americana

WURLITZER
JUKEBOX

A B C D E F G H J K L M N P Q R S T U V
1 2 3 4 5 6 7 8 9 0
WURLITZER
Americana

Atlanta
Wurlitzer

ATLANTA
Wurlitzer

WURLITZER

ATLANTA
Wurlitzer

Baltic

Baltic 3
WURLITZER
means Music to millions®

Baltic 4

WURLITZER
means Music to millions®

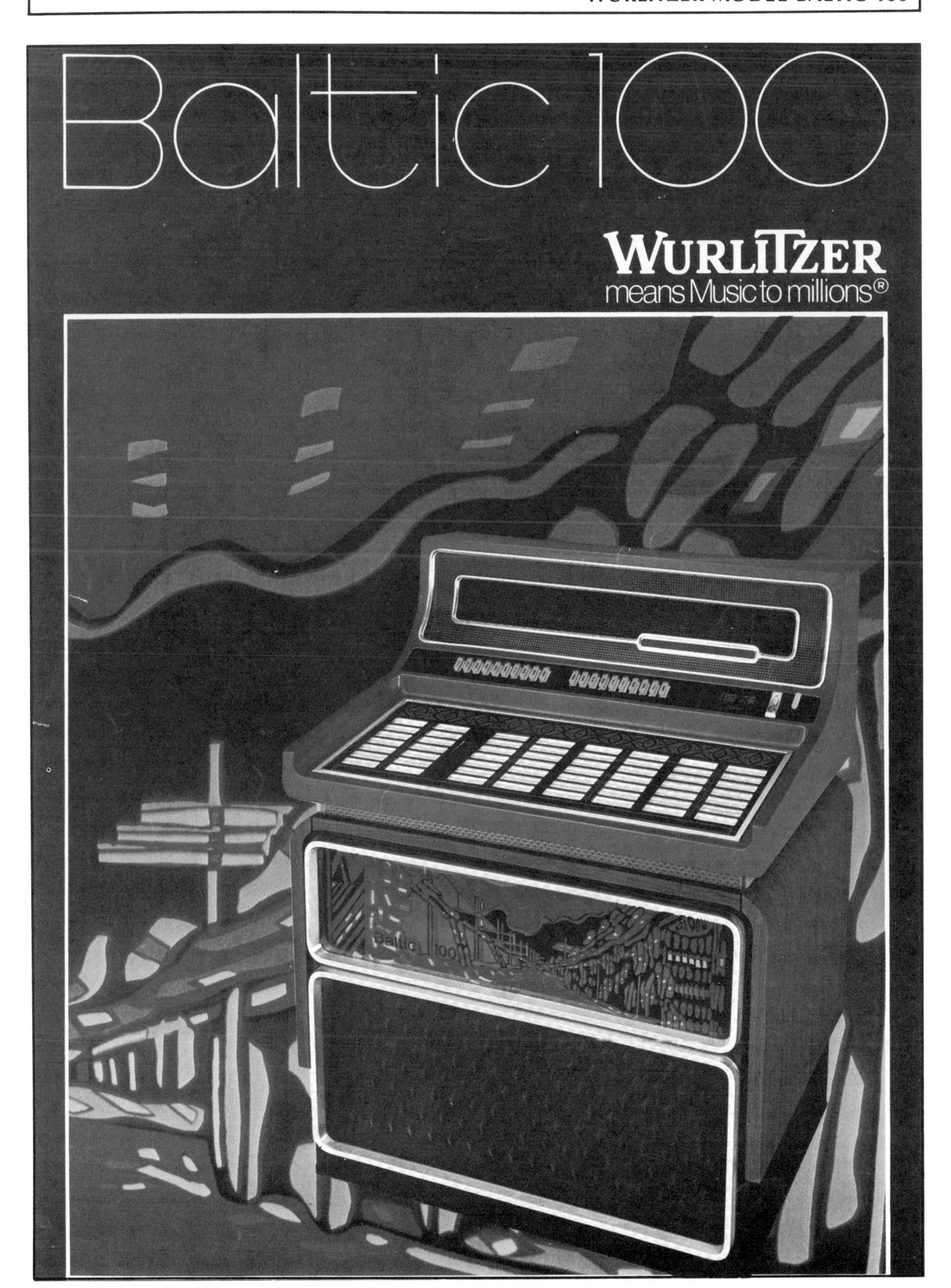
Baltic 100
WURLITZER
means Music to millions®
Baltic 100

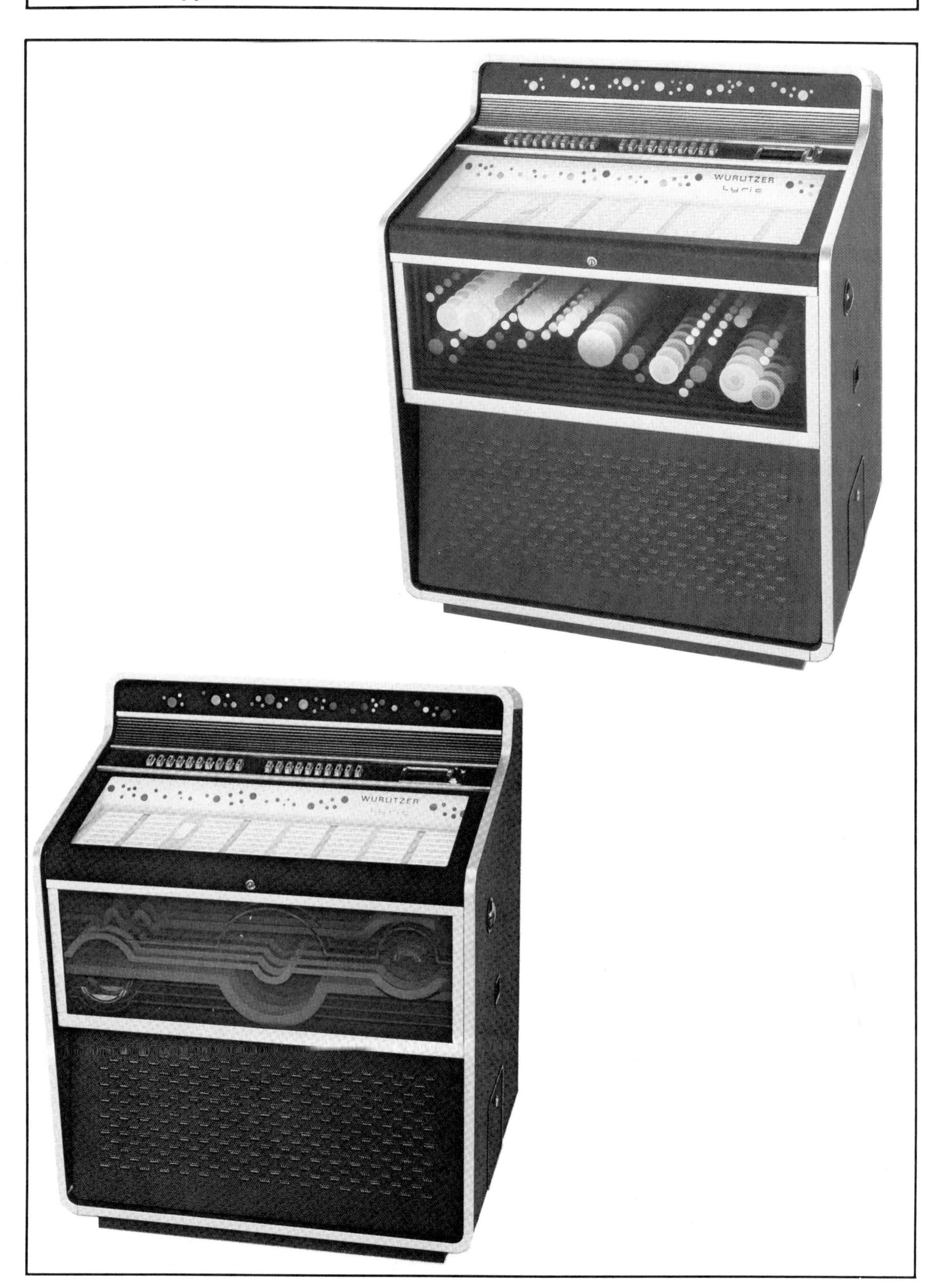
WURLITZER
Lyric
WURLITZER

Lyric
WURLITZER
means Music to millions®
WURLITZER
WURLITZER

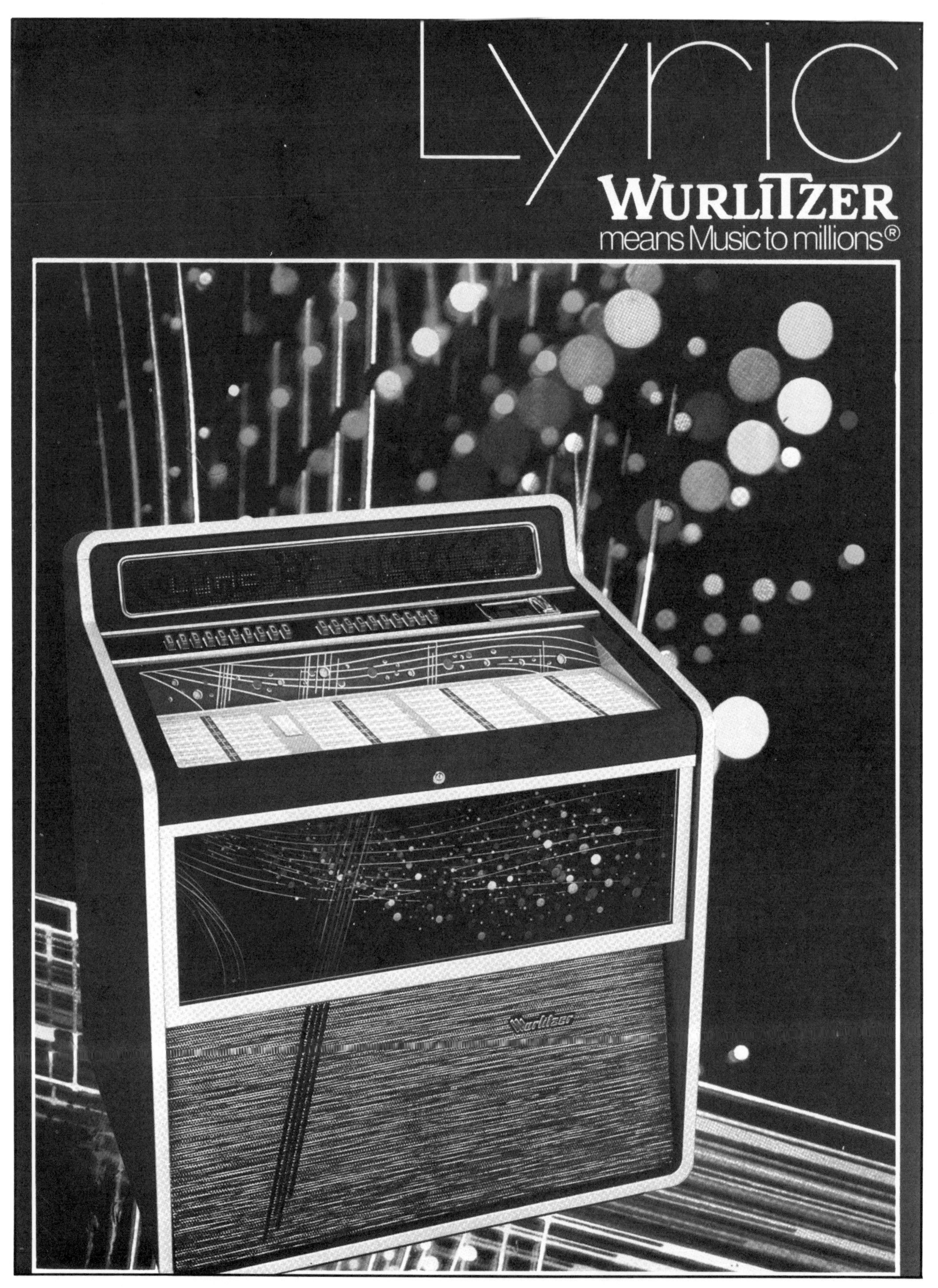
Lyric
WURLITZER
means Music to millions®
Wurlitzer

Wurlitzer

Tarock
WURLITZER
means Music to millions®

TAROCK (1982-84)

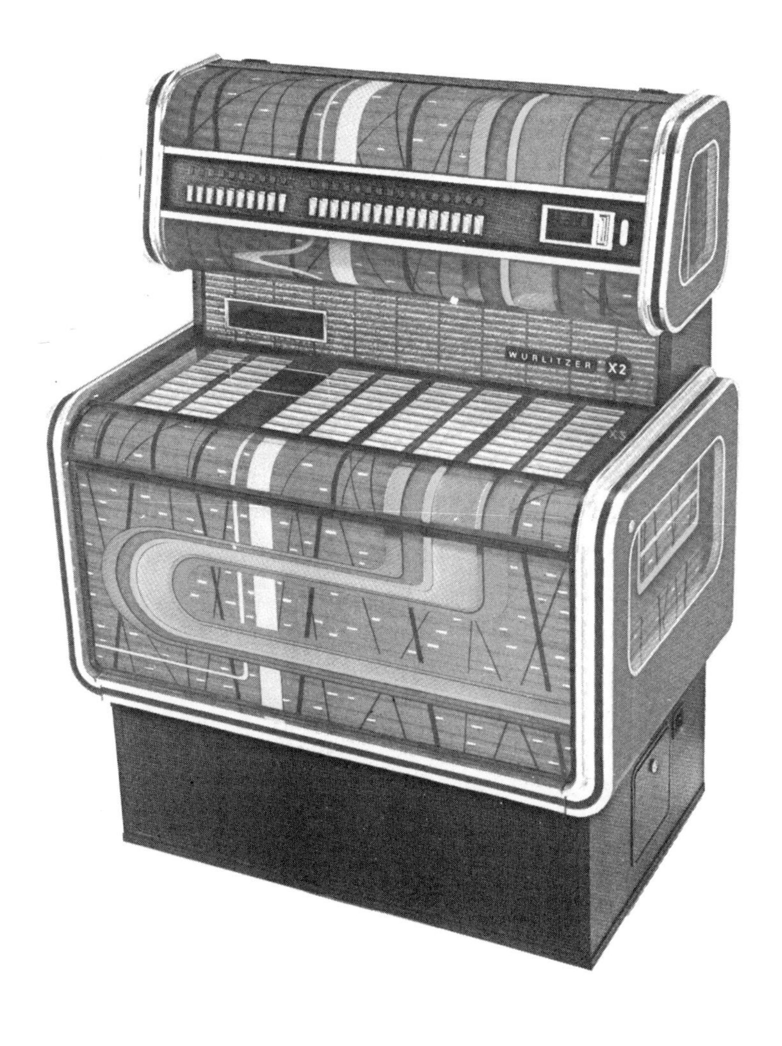
WURLITZER X2

Cabaret
WURLITZER
means Music to millions®

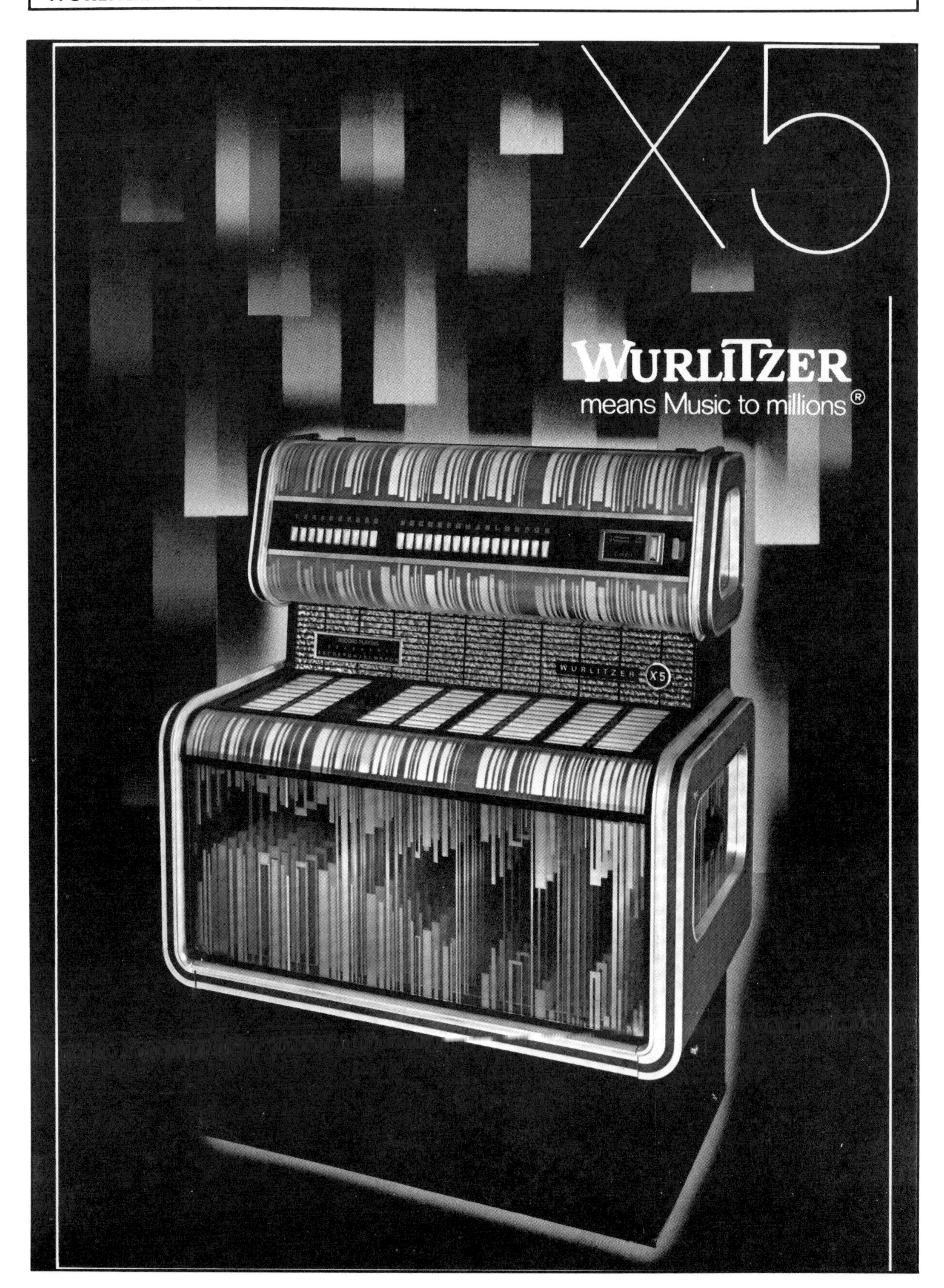
X5
WURLITZER
means Music to millions®
WURLITZER X5

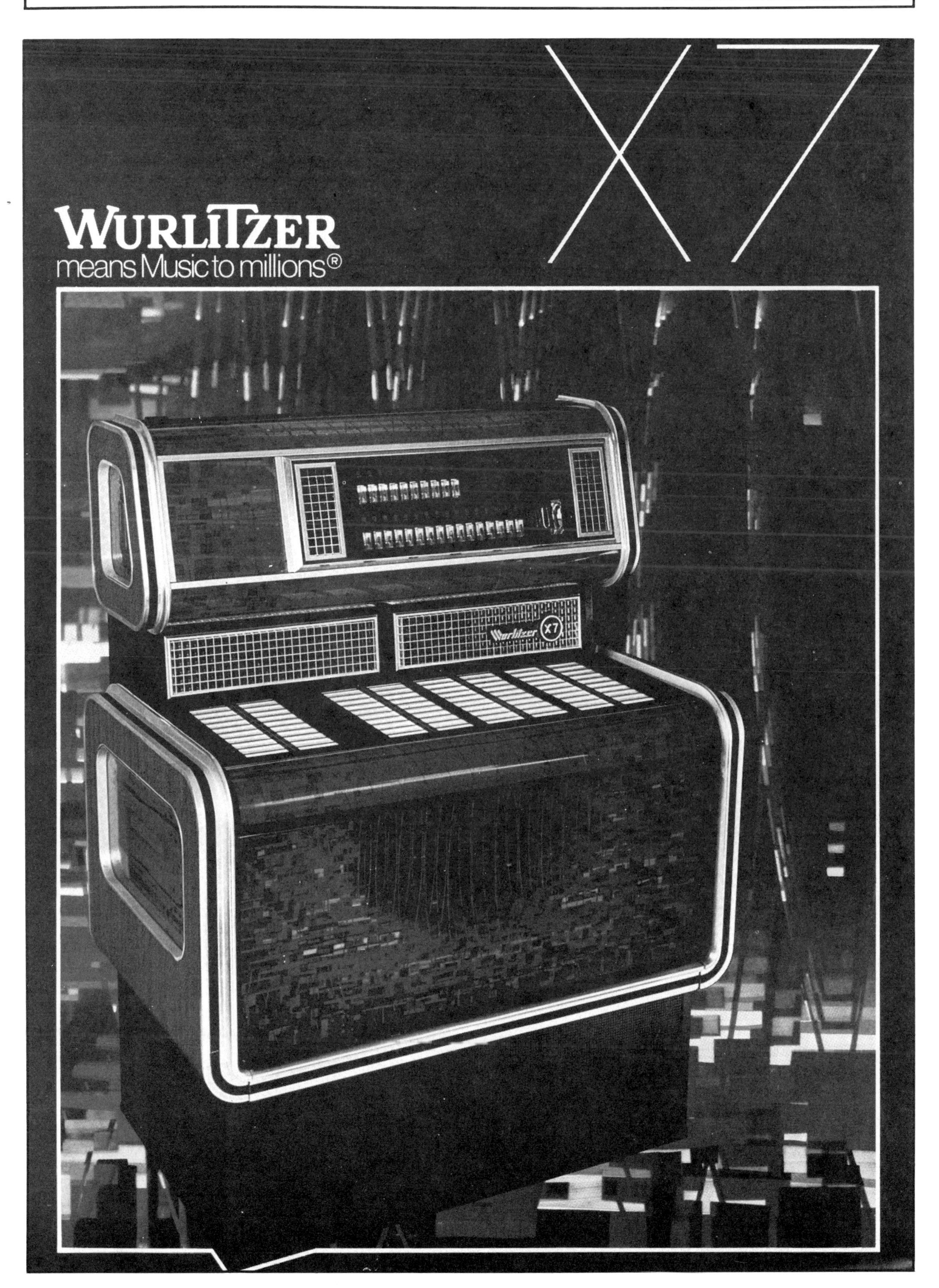
X7
WURLITZER
means Music to millions®
Wurlitzer
X7

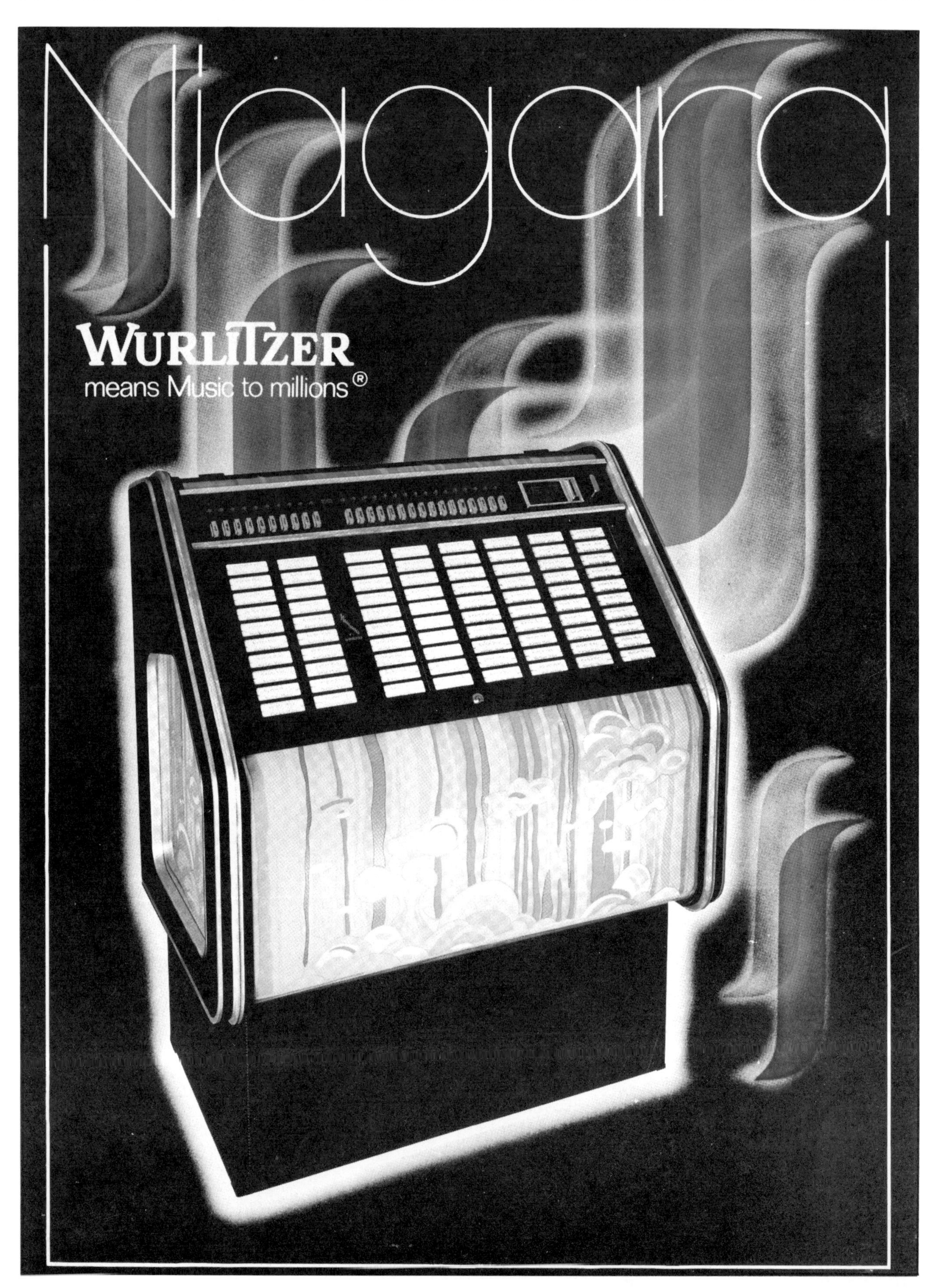
Niagara
WURLITZER
means Music to millions®

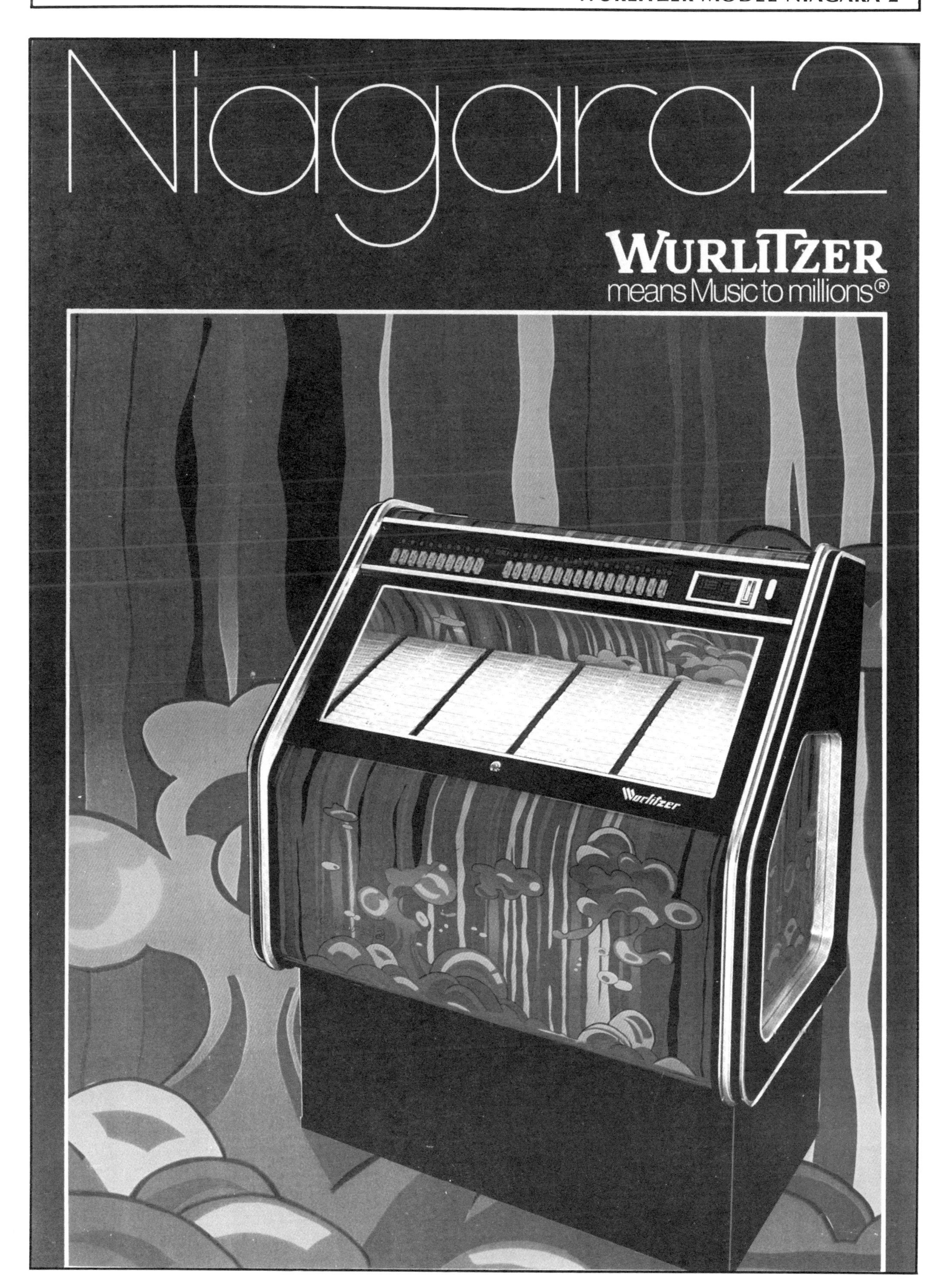
Niagara 2
WURLITZER
means Music to millions®
Wurlitzer

Wurlitzer
NIAGARA

Niagara
WURLITZER
means Music to millions®
electronic
Wurlitzer

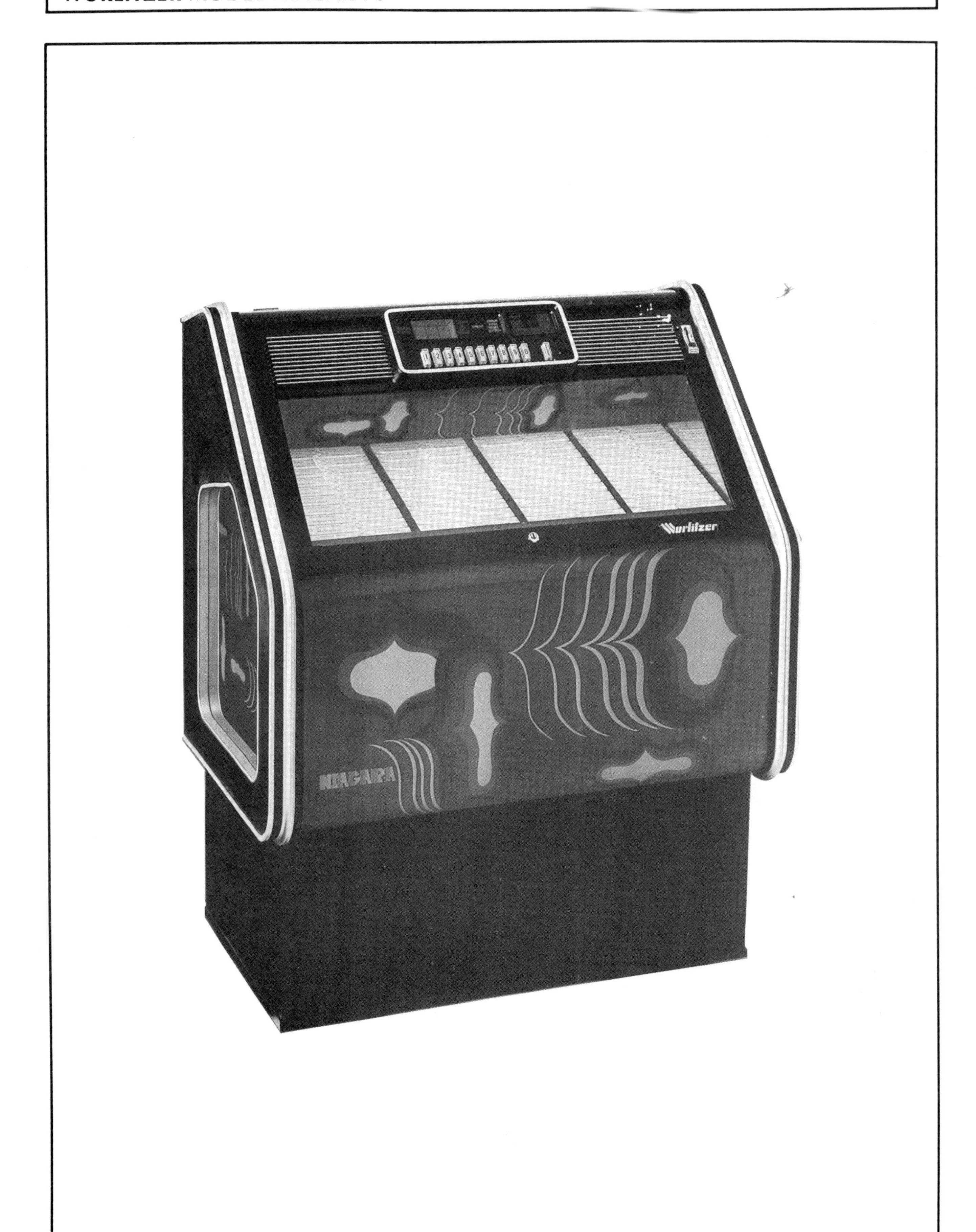
Wurlitzer
NIAGARA

Wurlitzer

Carillon
Wurlitzer

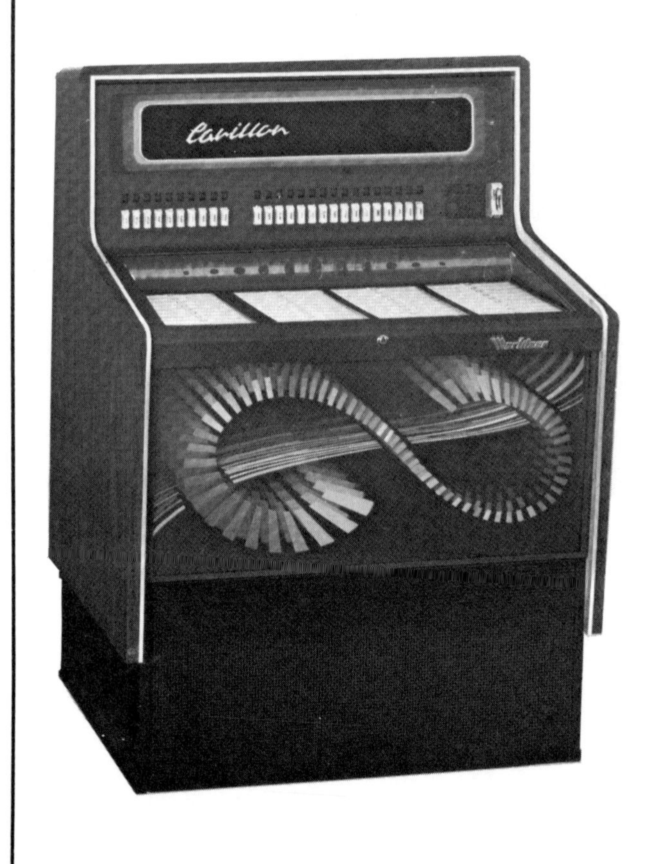
Carillon
Wurlitzer

Wurlitzer
Silhouette

Wurlitzer
Silhouette

WURLITZER MODEL ESTRELLA

Caravelle

Wurlitzer
Fuego

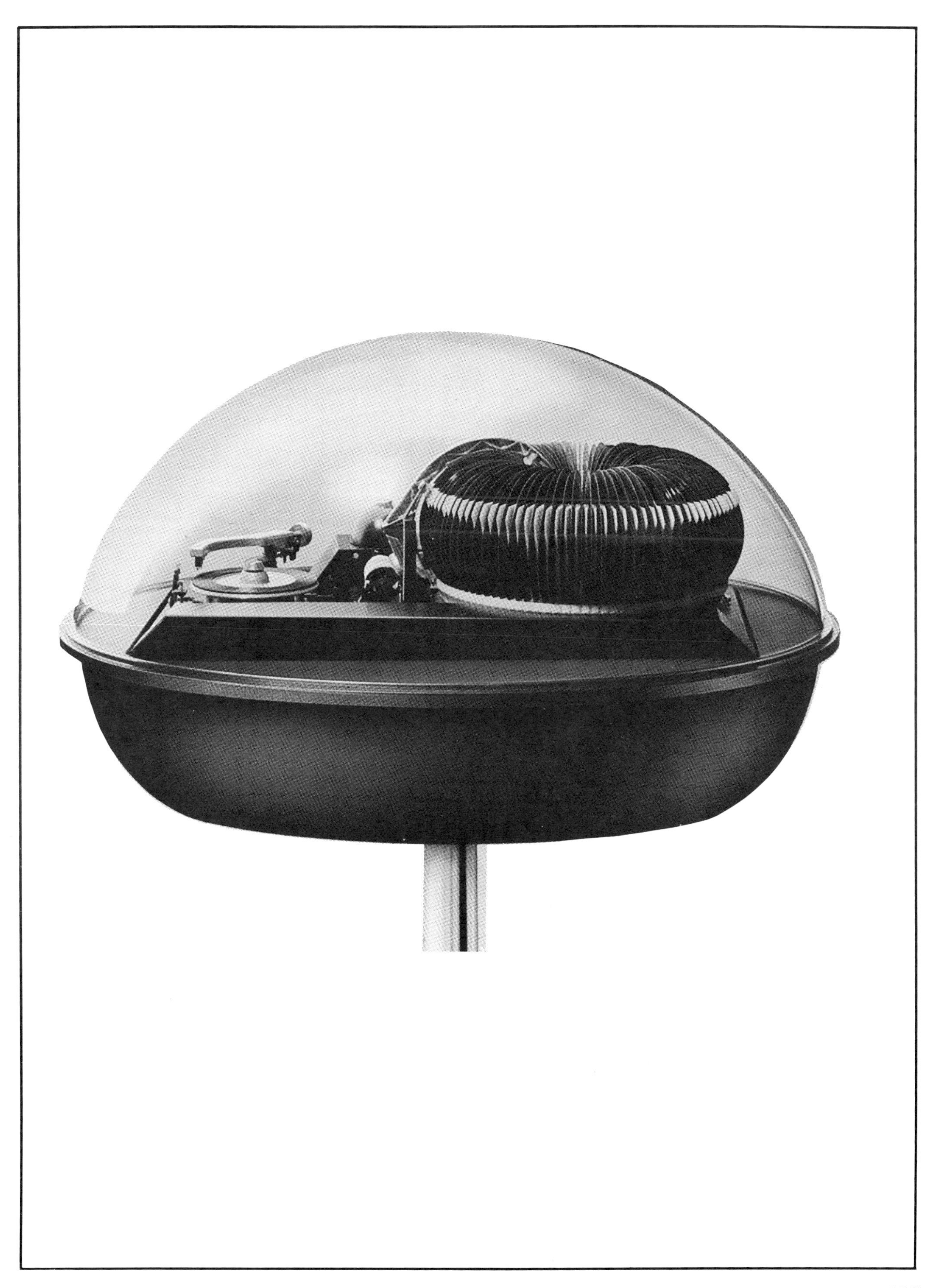

WURLITZER MODEL SL 700

Wurlitzer
Diana

A COMPLETE IDENTIFICATION GUIDE TO THE WURLITZER JUKEBOX

Only through the co-operation of Wurlitzer, who furnished the photographs and statistics, was this book possible. This book covers all the Wurlitzer jukeboxes, from 1934-1984. Each machine has its own $8\frac{1}{2}$ x 11 page. Some of the photos are rare and some have never been published before. With an easy to use reference list and the large pictures, you should be able to identify ANY Wurlitzer jukebox.
IBSN 0-912789-01-8 Softbound, $12.95

JUKEBOX RESTORATION

Restoration articles, tips and techniques taken from the "Jukebox Collector Newsletter" and "Victory Glass Newsletter" are a large part of this book. If you want a quick education about jukeboxes, then you need a copy of this book.
ISBN 0-912789-00-X Softbound $11.95

JUKEBOX COLLECTOR NEWSLETTER

The inexpensive classified ads section (10¢ per word) is where almost everyone turns to when they get their copy of JC. After that, then its time to read the display ads for new products or for any good deals on parts or jukeboxes. Victory Glass Co., Antique Apparatus, Golden Age Jukebox Co., Jukebox Junkyard, Orange Trading Co., Jukebox Junction, Home Arcade, Keith Electronics, SRS "The Speaker Shop", RAF Collections, Ron Shaw, Ray Eklund, Lloyd Spangler, Loose Change and AMR Publishing are some of the regular display advertisers. The rest of the newsletter is filled out with articles and news. I know all the coin-op publications and you can't find a better publication than JC for jukebox information. JC is published every month & on time, to keep you better informed and a step ahead of your friends.

12 months for $20
6 months for $11
Sample copy $2

FROM TIN FOIL TO STEREO

This is a book that every phonograph collector should read. 550 pages of history and valuable information about the phonograph make it "The reference book".
ISBN 0-672-212206-4 Hardbound $20

JUKEBOX: THE GOLDEN AGE

If you want excellent color photos of jukeboxes and can only afford 1 book, this is the book to buy. Over 65 pictures in color of our favorite jukeboxes. The hardbound edition is now out of print and not many hardbound copies are around so don't wait too long to get this one.
ISBN 0-89581-035-2 Hardbound $13
ISBN 0-399-50844-9 Softbound $8

AMERICAN PREMIUM GUIDE TO COIN-OPERATED MACHINES

This fully illustrated guide was compiled by one of the country's foremost collectors and restorers of coin-operated machines. Jukeboxes, slot machines, gumballs and trade stimulators are described and valued.
ISBN 0-89689-024-4 Softbound $10

THE OFFICIAL VICTORY GLASS PRICE GUIDE TO ANTIQUE JUKEBOXES 1984-85

This book includes the first grading system devised to more accurately judge your jukebox. With 50 illustrations, over 1,000 prices on over 200 models (1959 & older) it will give you all the information you need in judging and pricing a jukebox.
ISBN 0-930181-00-X Softbound $10

WURLITZER 1015 SERVICE INSTRUCTIONS AND PARTS CATALOG

If you own a Wurlitzer 1015 or are thinking about buying a 1015, then you should have this book. It has service instructions, a parts catalog and wiring diagrams.
ISBN 0-912789-02-6 Softbound $12

ROCK-OLA 1422 SERVICE MANUAL

The model 1422, 1426 & 1428 Rock-Ola jukeboxes can be serviced with this manual. It includes service instruction, parts listings and amplifier schematics for these machines.

Softbound $8

THE WURLITZER PHONOGRAPH COMPANYS "BROWN BOOK"

Wurlitzer, Seeburg, Rock-Ola, Aireon, AMI Packard, Mills and Filben 1948 models are compared. Comparative photos, dimensions and retail prices of these manufacturers phonographs speakers and wallboxes. Not pictured in photograph.

Softbound $:

ENAMELED PINS

These pins are very attractive and colorful. Wome especially, just love them. Thousands have been sol already. The models available now: Rock-Ola 1428 Wurlitzer 750, 850, Johnny-1-Note, 1015, & 950.

Postpaid, $5 or your choice of any 3 for $1

ORDER FROM -----> JUKEBOX COLLECTOR NEWSLETTER
2545 SE 60TH CT
DES MOINES, IA 50317-5099 <----- ORDER FROM

JUKEBOX 78'S
Volume I or II

Each set of records is a 25 record collection of 50 all-time favorites. 50's and 60's tunes by the original artists. Elvis, Buddy Holly, Little Richard and Danny & The Juniors to name a few. Ideal for use on your classic 78 jukeboxes. Send a SASE for the complete list of Volume I & Volume II.

Postpaid, each set $125

CAUDLE LITHOGRAPH PRINT

This lithograph print is undoubtly one of the best you'll ever find of a jukebox. It is on heavy, glossy paper. The heavy paper makes it durable and the glossiness makes the chome on the 1015 really shine. This print is 17" wide and 22" high. Put it in a nice frame and stand back for all the nice comments you'll get on your new acquisition. This lithograph is available in art stores for $19.95 but I'm making it available to you for only-

Postpaid, $12.95 or 2 copies for $19.95

EMBROIDERED PATCHES

These are real eye catchers with their vivid colors. Hundreds have been sewn on jackets & shirts or used in a display. I promise, you won't be disappointed in this beauty. The Wurlitzer 1015 patch is pictured, but a 850 & Victory patch is also available. $5\frac{1}{2}$" wide by $9\frac{1}{2}$" tall.

Postpaid, $12.50

JUKEBOX SATURDAY NIGHT

This comprehensive book not only covers the history of the jukebox companies, its pages are covered with many pictures. This highly sought after book is nearly sold-out. 20,000 copies were printed but less than 400 copies remain in dealers hands. So act now or you'll be crying your eyes out later.

Softbound $25

WURLITZER 1934-1974

Reprinted from original Wurlitzer brochures, this book pictures many Wurlitzer jukeboxes, speakers and wallboxes. Why risk damage to your original literature when you can have all this in one 238 page book. You could even loan it to a friend!

ISBN 0-913599-19-0 Deluxe hardcover style $27

Paperback style $19

ORDER FROM -----> JUKEBOX COLLECTOR NEWSLETTER
2545 SE 60TH CT.
DES MOINES, IA 50317-5099 <----- ORDER FROM

WURLITZER SERVICE AND PARTS MANUALS
*All the Manuals are professional reprints, not Xerox copies.

Distributor
Jukebox Collector
2545 SE 60th Ct.
Des Moines, Iowa 50317

W-4. P-10 and P-12 Service Manual 90 pages........ $24.50
W-5. P-10, P-12, P-30, P-400, 312, 412, 35, 400 Parts Catalog.
Also limited reference to the 316, 416 and 716 74 pages........ $21.50
W-6. 312, 412 and 35 Service Manual 114 pages........ $32.50
W-7. 24 and 24-A Service Manual 125 pages........ $22.50
W-8. 24 and 24-A Parts Catalog 70 pages........ $20.00
W-11. P-500, G-500, P-500A, G-500A, 600, 600A Parts Catalog 123 pages........ $24.50
W-13. 700 and 800 Parts Catalog 98 pages........ $22.50
W-17. 500, 500A, 600, 600A, K-600, K-600A, 750, 750-E, 780, 780-E,
700, 800 Service Manual 174 pages........ $16.50
*This is an excellent manual at a SUPER PRICE!
W-21. 1015 Service Manual and Parts Catalog 96 pages........ $11.95
W-23. 1017 Hideaway Service Manual and Parts Catalog 152 pages........ $17.50
W-24. 1080 Parts Catalog 78 pages........ $17.50
For Service Manual, use 1015 Service Manual.
W-27. 1100 Service Manual and Parts Catalog 134 pages........ $16.50
W-28. 1250 Service Manual and Parts Catalog 96 pages........ $21.50
W-29. 1400 and 1450 Service Manual and Parts Catalog 135 pages........ $27.50
W-32. 1500A and 1550A Service and Parts Manual 118 pages........ $27.50
W-33. 1600, 1650, 1600A and 1650A Service and Parts Manual 150 pages........ $32.50
W-35. 1700 and 1700HF Service and Parts Manual 166 pages........ $32.50
W-36. 1800 Service and Parts Manual 166 pages........ $32.50
W-37. 1900 Service and Parts Manual 112 pages........ $26.50
W-38. 2000 Service and Parts Manual 100 pages........ $24.50
W-39. 2100 Service and Parts Manual 119 pages........ $27.50
W-40. 2104 Service and Parts Manual 102 pages........ $24.50
W-41 2150 Service and Parts Manual 115 pages........ $27.50
W-42. 2200 Service and Parts Manual 93 pages........ $22.50
W-43. 2250 Service and Parts Manual 131 pages........ $29.50
W-44. 2300, 2310, 2300S, 2310S Service and Parts Manual 124 pages........ $27.50
W-45. 2304 and 2304S Service and Parts Manual 98 pages........ $24.50
W-46. 2400 Series, Service and Parts Manual 150 pages........ $32.50
W-47. 2500 Series, Service and Parts Manual 128 pages........ $29.50
W-48. 2600 Series, Service and Parts Manual 121 pages........ $29.50
W-49. 2700 Series, Service and Parts Manual 124 pages........ $29.50
W-50. 2800 Series, Service and Parts Manual 141 pages........ $32.50
W-51. 2900 Series, Service and Parts Manual 144 pages........ $32.50
W-52. 3000 Series, Supplement Manual 62 pages........ $21.50
For Service Manual, use 2900 Service Manual.
Buy W-51 and W-52 combined into 1 Manual for the price of........ $45.00
W-53. 3100 Series, Service and Parts Manual 120 pages........ $29.50
W-54. 3200 Series, Service and Parts Manual 124 pages........ $29.50
W-55. 3300 Series, Service and Parts Manual 122 pages........ $29.50
W-56. 3400 Series, Service and Parts Manual 150 pages........ $32.50
W-57. 3500 Series, Service and Parts Manual 160 pages........ $32.50
W-58. 3600 Series, Service and Parts Manual 124 pages........ $29.50
W-59. 3700 Series, Service and Parts Manual 136 pages........ $29.50
W-60. 1050 Service Supplement Manual 76 pages........ $24.50
For Service Manual, use 3700 Service Manual.
Buy W-59 and W-60 combined into 1 Manual for the price of........ $45.00
W-00. 3800 Series, Service and Parts Manual 133 pages........ $29.50

COUNTER-TOP MODELS

W-61. 50, 51, 61 Service Manual and Parts Catalog 192 pages........ $29.50
W-64. 41 and 71 Parts Catalog 52 pages........ $15.00
81 and 71 parts are interchangeable with a few exceptions.
*No Service Manuals for 41, 71, and 81 were ever issued.

ORDER FROM	
JUKEBOX COLLECTOR NEWSLETTER	NAME ____________
2545 SE 60TH CT	STREET ____________
DES MOINES, IA 50317-5099	CITY ____________
515-265-8324	STATE ______ ZIP ______
	PHONE # ____________

QTY.	DESCRIPTION		TOTAL
	A Complete Identification Guide To The Wurlitzer Jukebox	$12.95	
	Jukebox Restoration	$11.95	
	Jukebox Collector Newsletter - 1 year subscription	$20.00	PP
	Jukebox Collector Newsletter - 6 month subscription	$11.00	PP
	Jukebox Collector Newsletter - Sample copy	$2.00	PP
	From Tin Foil To Stereo	$20.00	
	Jukebox: The Golden Age	Hardbound $13.00	
	Jukebox: The Golden Age	Softbound $8.00	
	American Premium Guide to Coin-Operated Machines	$10.00	
	The Official Victory Glass Price Guide to Antique Jukeboxes 1984-85	$10.00	
	Wurlitzer 1015 Service Instructions & Parts Catalog	$12.00	
	Rock-Ola 1422 Service Manual	$8.00	
	The Wurlitzer Phonograph Companys' "Brown Book"	$5.00	
	Enameled pins	$5 or your choice of any 3 for $10.00	PP
	____Rock-Ola 1428, ____Johny-1-Note ____Wurlitzer 750, ____850, ____1015, ____950		
	Jukebox 78's Volume I	$125.00	PP
	Jukebox 78's Volume II	$125.00	PP
	Caudle Lithograph Print	$12.95 or 2 copies for $19.95	PP
	Embroidered Patches	$12.50	PP
	____Wurlitzer 1015, ____850, ____Victory		
	Jukebox Saturday Night	$25.00	
	Wurlitzer 1934-1974	Deluxe hardcover style $27.00	
	Wurlitzer 1934-1974	Paperback style $19.00	
	Shipping: For EACH BOOK add $1.00		
	Iowa Residents add 4% sales tax		
	TOTAL		

master charge

VISA

☐ MASTERCARD ☐ VISA

____

Signature of card holder
Minimum order $25 on credit card orders

______________________ ________

Account number Exp. Date

ORDERING INFORMATION

SHIPPING: PP=Postpaid. On shipments outside USA you pay actual shipping cost. Use your charge card or write for estimate of shipping cost.

PAYMENT: Checks (payment in US dollars on US bank). VISA OR MASTERCARD ($25 minimum).

SATISFACTION GUARANTEED ON ANY PURCHASE!

ORDER FROM	
JUKEBOX COLLECTOR NEWSLETTER 2545 SE 60TH CT DES MOINES, IA 50317-5099 515-265-8324	NAME ____________________ STREET ____________________ CITY ____________________ STATE __________ ZIP __________ PHONE # ______________

QTY.	DESCRIPTION		TOTAL
	A Complete Identification Guide To The Wurlitzer Jukebox	$12.95	
	Jukebox Restoration	$11.95	
	Jukebox Collector Newsletter - 1 year subscription	$20.00	PP
	Jukebox Collector Newsletter - 6 month subscription	$11.00	PP
	Jukebox Collector Newsletter - Sample copy	$2.00	PP
	From Tin Foil To Stereo	$20.00	
	Jukebox: The Golden Age	Hardbound $13.00	
	Jukebox: The Golden Age	Softbound $8.00	
	American Premium Guide to Coin-Operated Machines	$10.00	
	The Official Victory Glass Price Guide to Antique Jukeboxes 1984-85	$10.00	
	Wurlitzer 1015 Service Instructions & Parts Catalog	$12.00	
	Rock-Ola 1422 Service Manual	$8.00	
	The Wurlitzer Phonograph Companys' "Brown Book"	$5.00	
	Enameled pins	$5 or your choice of any 3 for $10.00	PP
	____Rock-Ola 1428, ____Johny-1-Note ____Wurlitzer 750, ____850, ____1015, ____950		
	Jukebox 78's Volume I	$125.00	PP
	Jukebox 78's Volume II	$125.00	PP
	Caudle Lithograph Print	$12.95 or 2 copies for $19.95	PP
	Embroidered Patches	$12.50	PP
	____Wurlitzer 1015, ____850, ____Victory		
	Jukebox Saturday Night	$25.00	
	Wurlitzer 1934-1974	Deluxe hardcover style $27.00	
	Wurlitzer 1934-1974	Paperback style $19.00	

Shipping: For EACH BOOK add $1.00	
Iowa Residents add 4% sales tax	
TOTAL	

☐ MASTERCARD ☐ VISA

____

Signature of card holder
Minimum order $25 on credit card orders

____________________ ________

Account number Exp. Date

ORDERING INFORMATION

SHIPPING: PP=Postpaid. On shipments outside USA you pay actual shipping cost. Use your charge card or write for estimate of shipping cost.

PAYMENT: Checks (payment in US dollars on US bank). VISA OR MASTERCARD ($25 minimum).

SATISFACTION GUARANTEED ON ANY PURCHASE!